Honours versus Money

Honours versus Money

The Economics of Awards

Bruno S. Frey and Jana Gallus

OXFORD
UNIVERSITY PRESS

Great Clarendon Street, Oxford, OX2 6DP,
United Kingdom

Oxford University Press is a department of the University of Oxford.
It furthers the University's objective of excellence in research, scholarship,
and education by publishing worldwide. Oxford is a registered trade mark of
Oxford University Press in the UK and in certain other countries

© Bruno Frey and Jana Gallus 2017

The moral rights of the authors have been asserted

First Edition published in 2017
Impression: 1

Published in the United States of America by Oxford University Press
198 Madison Avenue, New York, NY 10016, United States of America

British Library Cataloguing in Publication Data
Data available

Library of Congress Control Number: 2017932969

ISBN 978-0-19-879850-7

Printed in Great Britain by
Clays Ltd, St Ives plc

Preface

People are not only motivated by money. The desire to be recognized is a fundamental trait of human beings. Awards are well suited to fulfil this desire. For time immemorial, an innumerable variety of awards have existed in all countries and spheres of life.

Monarchs as well as presidents of republican countries bequeath orders and medals, such as the Order of the Garter given by the British Queen or the Presidential Medal of Freedom given by the American President. In the arts, the Man Booker Prize is given to writers, the Pritzker Prize to architects, the Oscars to film stars, the Grammy Awards to personalities in the music industry, and the Pulitzer Prize to journalists. The military abundantly use honours to remunerate and recognize soldiers and officers, including deceased ones. The Victoria Cross is a particularly important example, as it ranks on top of the honours system in the UK.

Awards are also most numerous in two areas where they would not necessarily be expected. In academia, where all that counts is expected to be the pursuit of knowledge, there are a great many awards. They range from honorary doctorates to the Nobel Prizes. Likewise, in business, money is taken to rule supreme. But in fact firms and other organizations hand out many different awards. The Employee of the Month or Manager of the Year are just two particularly well-known examples, but there are numerous other awards in the corporate sector.

In contrast to this obviously great importance stands the neglect of awards in economic science. The emphasis has for a long time been lying almost solely on monetary incentives, such as the various forms of pay-for-performance and bonuses. This may be attributed to the characteristics of monetary incentives, which are simple to administer, fungible for their recipients, and in line with the dominant commercialization of our contemporary societies.

But why are there so many awards? There is a straightforward answer. What human beings strongly strive for are honour, recognition, and attention. These desires are particularly well met by awards. When bequeathed, the recipients are explicitly and publicly lauded for their extraordinary achievements.

Our book analyses honours from an economic perspective, i.e. using economic theory and empirical methods. As far as we are aware, this is the first book offering a general analysis in this vein. It differs fundamentally from the science of orders and decoration, called phaleristics, as well as from historical and sociological treatises of the topic. We discuss the use of awards in different areas of society and explore the differences between awards and monetary compensation as well as other material and immaterial benefits. We integrate the economic analysis of awards into economic and business theory, including signalling and strategic management theory. Based on our own research, in which we empirically analyse the effects of honours on productivity in academia and the voluntary sector, we conclude that awards have great potential to significantly raise people's motivation and performance. Finally, we explore some of the areas and tasks where awards are particularly well suited, and where they may be superior to other motivators.

Our book intends to make a contribution to several literatures. After each chapter, we provide a brief discussion of the literature related to the specific topics covered.

- Honours add a so far largely neglected motivational instrument in addition to the monetary incentives intensively discussed in both economics and management science.

- Awards are well suited to raise intrinsic motivation, a crucial driving force in a modern economy, above and beyond extrinsic, material motivations. This enlarges the considerations made in social psychology and business economics, and more recently in economics.

- Academia bestows a great range of honours, including titles and distinguished fellowships. The corresponding analyses yield valuable insights for sociology and philosophy of science as well as for economics.

- The role and potential of awards in the voluntary sector are illuminated. This application is of considerable relevance for several disciplines, in particular sociology, social psychology, and social work.

- The effects of awards on subjective well-being inform the many variants of happiness research undertaken in psychology, economics, and management science.

This book builds on a series of articles, partly written together with Susanne Neckermann, Reto Cueni, Benno Torgler, and Ho Fai Chan. Parts of the work have previously been presented at universities and other scholarly institutions in Switzerland, Germany, Austria, France,

Denmark, the Netherlands, Spain, the United Kingdom, and the United States, as well as at numerous scholarly conferences in various countries.

We are grateful for comments received on several occasions by so many scholars that it is impossible to name them all. For the specific case of state orders, we had the unique opportunity to interview the late Professor Roman Herzog, former President of the Federal Republic of Germany, for which we are most grateful. We also greatly appreciate the insights provided by the Nobel Prize winners in Economics, Sir James Mirrlees and Joseph Stiglitz.

We moreover want to explicitly mention Bruce Ackerman, John Armour, Stephan Bechtold, Christine Benesch, Tim Besley, Trine Bille, Iris Bohnet, Bob Cooter, Reto Cueni, Giuseppe Dari-Mattiacci, Reiner Eichenberger, Christoph Engel, Lars Feld, Gerd Folkers, Robert Frank, René Frey, Jonas Friedrich, Victor Ginsburgh, Fernando Gomez, Andrew Guzman, Henry Hansmann, Dirk Helbing, Jürg Helbling, Gérard Hertig, Gebhard Kirchgässner, Kai Konrad, Lewis Kornhauser, Siegwart Lindenberg, Simon Lüchinger, Karl Ulrich Mayer, Stephan Meier, Felix Oberholzer-Gee, Karl-Dieter Opp, the late Elinor Ostrom, Andrew Oswald, Katharina Pistor, Susan Rose-Ackerman, Christoph Schaltegger, Friedrich Schneider, Hans-Werner Sinn, Lasse Steiner, Alois Stutzer, and Hannelore Weck-Hannemann. In particular, we thank Evelyn Holderegger and Jonas Friedrich for carefully checking the manuscript, and Margit Osterloh and Gregor Martynus for their continuous and wonderful psychic and practical support.

Contents

List of Figures

List of Tables

List of Tables

1

Why Awards?

Motivation by Money and by Honours

Top managers nowadays get paid astonishingly high bonuses and incomes. The average CEO compensation of the top 350 US firms was about $15 million in 2013. This is a staggering sum of money compared to what other CEOs get, not to speak of other employees. The CEO-to-worker compensation was 20-to-1 in 1965, peaked at 380-to-1 in 2000, and was around 300-to-1 in 2013 (Mishel and Davis 2014; Piketty 2014). However, on being asked, many CEOs emphasize that they are not primarily interested in the money. Rather, they take the huge sum as a sign of appreciation and recognition for their work. The benefit they derive from the bonus is mainly due to higher self-evaluation and, maybe even more importantly, the higher prestige and status gained compared with their colleagues and other top managers.

We argue in this book that there is a better alternative for showing appreciation to managers and other employees than heaping piles of money on them. Providing them with what everybody longs for but nobody can buy, honour and esteem. Awards cater especially to these values by explicitly and publicly praising the recipients for their achievements, and they do so at a much lower cost than bonus payments. Thanks to their public visibility, honours reduce the need to recur to conspicuous consumption to signal one's achievements.

Awards are expressions of appreciation that can take various forms, ranging from orders, crosses, medals, decorations, prizes, trophies, and certificates to honorific titles and other honours. They can be found in virtually all spheres of life (see Chapter 2). There are awards far beyond the political and military sectors: in the humanitarian sector, in architecture, arts (film, television, radio, dance, music, literature), design, education, journalism, advertising, games and sports, as well as in academia and business. Awards are not only widespread; they also have a long history.

Benefits from Honours

Honours create various social values.

Awards can Contribute to Happiness

Awards provide hedonic benefits to the winners and make them feel recognized and honoured, which can raise their subjective well-being. Contrary to most people's first intuition, that awards probably reduce the well-being of non-recipients, we want to point out that the opposite may also hold. The positive effect of awards can extend far beyond the individual winners, and apply to members of organizations or people living in cities receiving awards, as well as to people identifying with a specific cause or person being honoured (e.g. because they belong to the unit that gave rise to a 'superstar'). But awards may also produce negative external effects on persons envious of the recipients who have so far failed to be honoured.

Awards Raise Productivity and Contributions to Public Goods

Awards can be used to increase employees' productivity and engagement in their work. The givers hope to raise the performance of their organization by inducing the necessary changes in the behaviour of aspirants and the future behaviour of award winners.

Individuals not winning an award may hope to get the award in the future and therefore put in the effort desired by the giver. However, awards can also backfire when disgruntled non-recipients reduce their work effort or even resort to sabotage. It is important to recognize that, although providing honours may be 'cheap', it can have powerful effects on people's motivations.

Collecting Value

The insignia going with awards provide pleasure to collectors, especially in the case of orders, medals, crosses, and decorations. Collections can be based on a range of different objectives. They may be focused on orders of a particular period or country, or on a particular kind of order (e.g. those depicting a lion or an eagle), or they may be assembled with a view to the aesthetic qualities of the insignia.

Even for people who do not usually see themselves as collectors, receiving an award may trigger a desire to also get the other awards in order to complete what they see or what has been explicitly designed as sets. Awards that can trigger such motivations abound. An example is the Yelp Elite badge provided to top contributors to Yelp, an online crowd-sourced local business review site. The seemingly subtle decision to add the given year in which the badges were earned (depicted with small badges saying, e.g., Elite '16, '15, '14 on the contributor's profile page) can motivate recipients to exert effort to not lose their streak and win the badge in consecutive years as well.

Advantages of Honours

As we will argue and try to show in this book, purely symbolic awards have distinctive advantages over monetary compensation.

Awards have greater visibility than bonuses and other monetary rewards, which are normally undisclosed and not directly observed by others. In many cases employees are prohibited to reveal the bonuses they receive to their colleagues. In a survey undertaken in Germany (German Socio-Economic Panel 2016), 41 per cent of the respondents affirmed that it was not welcome in their enterprise to speak about incomes. Accordingly, 51 per cent indicated that there was no wage transparency among employees. The goal of expressing recognition to a person is far better reached by handing out an award than by just transferring money to an account. Awards are always given in front of an audience and often also draw media attention, which greatly pleases most people.

We posit that awards can crowd in the intrinsic work motivation of recipients. Award givers, when handing out the award in a public cere-mony, emphasize the particularly valuable contributions made by the recipient and often go to great lengths to highlight the recipient's expertise. In contrast, monetary rewards risk crowding out people's intrinsic motivations when they shift their focus to the money gained rather than the content of work. Monetary incentives often come along with increased efforts to monitor people's performance and, due to this sense of control, may undermine the inherent interest in the tasks at hand.

Awards are particularly well suited to honour comprehensive achieve-ments. The respective performance need only be specified in a broad way. This applies to the life achievement awards often bequeathed in culture and sports, as well as to early career awards that are based on a person's expected future trajectory rather than on past accomplish-ments. The awards discussed in this book mostly recognize performance that is difficult or impossible to exactly define and measure. Such vagueness is characteristic for qualified occupations in modern economies. Indeed, only simple work can be exactly identified and measured. Money forces the giver, if not to measure and quantify the underlying performance, then at the very least to put a precise value on it.

In order to express appreciation to managers it is often unclear whether a compensation of 10, 20, or 60 million euros would be appropriate. The amount is likely determined based on what other firms pay their managers, with the risk of inducing an upward spiral in bonus pay. As a consequence, the work of CEOs is compensated with ever-increasing sums of money, leading to a more and more unequal distribution of income and wealth. This may lead to social unrest and political instability. Public honours and recognition, we argue, are a means of breaking this unfortunate spiral.

Awards can strengthen people's commitment to the organization giving the award. The intrinsic motivation to perform well and in the interest of the employer is praised by the giver and hence reinforced. In contrast, when an attempt is made to measure performance by pay, this intrinsic work motivation may well be crowded out. After all, performance pay may inadvertently signal that the ultimate goal of all endeavours is to get money. All that matters is to reach the criteria in order to get the bonus promised. The content of work becomes secondary. They are induced to disregard everything not covered by the criteria imposed—even if they know this is bad for the organization they work for. Moreover, employees promised bonuses have a strong incentive to game the system. If shareholder value is used as the major criterion for CEOs, they may jack up this number by short-term manipulations or by buying back shares. The resulting shareholder value then does not reflect the underlying state of the corporation but may be biased in favour of short-run effects.

Awards establish a bond of loyalty between givers and recipients. This element of a social tie, which is based on trust, refers to both sides. The recipients, to some measure, accept the goals and intentions of the giver. Otherwise, they would be castigated for having agreed to receive the honour. The givers are also to some extent held accountable for the recipients' future activities, as they have considered the latter worthy of being honoured and have put their reputation on the line.

Awards can be used to structure and shape a field, as is the case for instance with the Academy Awards (Oscars), whose verdict of what is to be deemed high quality has had a great influence on the movie industry. In the reasons given for bequeathing an award, as well as in the ceremony accompanying the award's conferral, the givers communicate what is important to them, what should be achieved, and/or how this should be done. Bestowing an award allows givers to make such statements broadly visible. In that sense, awards have an expressive function that givers can exploit to communicate normative judgements. It would be difficult to do so merely by promising money. Bequeathing an award also provides a suitable opportunity for networking with people engaged in the same endeavour. They allow the in-group of award givers, sponsors, jury members, and recipients to extend and strengthen their relationships. As a result, joint actions can be undertaken, therewith furthering the goals of the award-giving organization.

Awards are a low-cost way to honour individuals as well as organizations and causes. The costs essentially consist in a piece of ribbon handed over at an award ceremony. While such ceremonies may take an opulent form (such as in the case of Nobel Prizes), awards are often bestowed in the context of another event that primarily serves another goal (as is the case for an employee award bequeathed at the general assembly).

Awards are often not subject to taxation. In contrast, monetary bonuses and other material rewards and fringe benefits—such as expensive company cars or luxurious apartments—are taxed. This is most relevant for award recipients when the marginal tax rate on the highest incomes is around 90 per cent, as used to be the case in the 1960s and 1970s in the United States and elsewhere, for instance in Sweden. For managers to insist on another million when 900,000 US dollars end up with the tax office is not attractive. Their status would better be served by receiving a prestigious business award.

Another reason for bequeathing awards is the private benefits gained by the decision-makers in the award-giving institutions. The media and the social attention gained raise their status in society and among peers, making them important personalities. In the case of famous recipients, award givers also share in their glory if the recipients accept the award. For famous and well-regarded personalities, this creates the challenge of finding a way to sort through and politely refuse some of the honours they are being offered.

These characteristics of awards put honours in contrast to mere pay raises. Income, of course, is a necessary part of work and a strong motivator, and cannot be dispensed with. However, we will argue that just relying on money to foster the work motivation of employees is a mistaken approach. It is subject to strongly diminishing returns. For the super rich, to take an extreme example, the extra 60 million euros (or 48 million British pounds) do not as such provide sufficient motivation to raise their work effort. Beneficiaries of high salaries regularly acknowledge this limitation of monetary rewards. They invariably claim to have worked at maximum intensity also when their salary was much lower.

Monetary bonuses have over the past few years come under strong attack in the popular media as well as among scholars (Bénabou and Tirole 2016). In the top echelons of many parts of society, including the financial and corporate sectors, medical professions, and sports, pay to those at the top has literally exploded. This has led to grave concerns about the increasingly unequal distribution of incomes in society. Private sector representatives have typically argued that such high pay is necessary to attract, motivate, and retain 'talent' and 'high performers'. But at the same time, such wage explosion has been accompanied by malfeasance and moral hazard. As a result, corporations have incurred reputational damage, plummeting demand, and falling stock values. Some firms with particularly highly paid top executives have been subjected to high fines, or have gone bankrupt. Such extreme bidding for (presumed) talent risks destroying work ethics and reduces social welfare. Therefore, other incentive systems should be carefully considered. Our book argues that public recognition in the form of awards can play an important role as a valuable alternative to excessive monetary pay.

The positive effects of getting an award on motivation also apply to honours outside the employment relationship, such as state orders. In the cases in which awards are bestowed for a person's lifetime achievement, the prize has little or no effect on the future performance of the award recipients. Rather, it can legitimize the field or cause the giver stands for, and it can also serve to create role models and incentives for others hoping to receive similar distinction in the future.

Other Motivators

Besides honours there are other alternatives to using money as a reward (see Figure 1.1). And even money can be used as a signal of appreciation. One alternative to monetary incentives and awards is praise or positive feedback given to individuals acting in a way the giver deems desirable. For personal praise, the status effect and the attention received in the

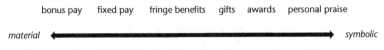

Figure 1.1 The nature of rewards

general public are low or do not exist at all. While this is a form of appreciation valued by the recipients, it has little or no visibility among co-workers and the public at large. Moreover, personal praise and private feedback do not serve superiors to establish role models whose behaviour others may endeavour to emulate. There is also the danger that personal praise as well as awards are distributed too liberally among members of an organization, in particular where the set of members is clearly defined and rather small. In the case of awards and other positional goods, to retain their value, the number of persons being publicly awarded has to be restricted.

Another motivator is gifts given to those employees considered to work well and in the interest of the organization. Gift giving confronts the giver with a problem similar to that encountered with monetary pay, the determination of the appropriate size and value of the gift to match the services performed. It is noteworthy that in almost all societies an effort is made to conceal the price paid for gifts. This moves gifts closer to awards, which have little monetary value as such and are appreciated mainly for their symbolic content.

Figure 1.1 shows how awards fit into the various incentives ranging from purely material (bonus pay) to purely immaterial (personal praise). All these motivators are extrinsic, i.e. influence behaviour from outside, in contrast to intrinsic motivation that comes from inside the person and work design.

Gifts are inefficient in the sense that the recipients, if given the cash equivalent of the gift, would find more efficient uses for the money (except in the rare cases where the giver exactly fulfils the wishes of the gift recipient). However, gifts can be employed to motivate employees, in particular if they signal that higher-ups have made an effort to personalize them. In contrast to money, and much similar to awards, gifts are often tangible and can serve as reminders of the recognition received. Holidays paid for by the company also create lasting memories, just like award ceremonies do. The effects on motivation can thus be more sustained than in the case of money, where people may forget (or not even see) the exact amount received in their bank account. In many cases, bonuses are taken to be a regular part of compensation and therefore create expectations that imply they are no longer considered an extraordinary and memorable event. This may create negative effects on motivation and behaviour when the expected bonus or salary increase is no longer forthcoming.

Employees can also be motivated to perform in the interest of an organization by punishing deviant behaviour. In most if not all societies, this approach has been extensively used, as the respective criminal law codes show. Such negative sanctions often endeavour to closely monitor and steer human behaviour, but it is well known that this is possible only to a limited extent. People can invest a lot of effort and originality in circumventing and cheating on laws and regulations. Tax fraud is a case in point; it has always existed and will probably always exist. To react by increasing punishment is only partly effective, as this induces people to move to yet other, and even more difficult to detect, areas in order to circumvent the fines. There is an important negative consequence of forcing people to act in a particular way by threatening punishment. Intrinsic motivation is crowded out as it becomes unnecessary. Commitment, trust, and loyalty are lost, though they are of crucial importance in all societies, in particular in modern ones based on a large measure of independence at work.

Conclusions

Being recognized and held in esteem by others is an important concern for many people. Award giving is in many respects ideal to cater to this desire. Honours are well suited to convey appreciation for achievement, and they may be better at this than monetary compensation. Awards are valuable motivators when performance can only be vaguely determined and measured; when commitment, mutual trust, and loyalty are particularly important; and when it is advantageous to shape the direction of a field and create role models.

Awards can be expected to play a particularly important role in fields where performance is difficult to define, observe, and evaluate, such as the arts and knowledge work based on complex tasks. However, the number of awards has to be kept limited for them to remain valuable, and so (potential) award givers may find it useful to use awards as a complement to other motivators, such as praise, gifts, and money—all of which have distinctive advantages and drawbacks.

Related Literature

There is an important literature documenting the huge compensation received by top managers as well as the resulting gap to average worker salaries, and the rising inequality in society; see, e.g., Piketty and Saez (2003, 2013), or Bebchuk and Fried's (2004) book on *Pay without Performance: The Unfulfilled Promise of Executive Compensation*. The trend of an ever-increasing inequality of incomes and wealth in recent years is argued and documented in Piketty's (2014) *Capital in the Twenty-First Century*. In a research paper titled 'Bonus Culture: Competitive Pay, Screening, and Multitasking', Bénabou and Tirole (2016) carefully study the relationships between economic competition, excessive managerial pay, and the loss of intrinsic motivation and corporate ethics.

The ubiquity of awards is documented in Frey (2005), Best (2011), Neckermann and Frey (2013), and Gallus and Frey (2016a). A general overview of awards in historical perspective is given in the book by English (2005). The function of awards in structuring a field is studied in Anand and Watson (2004), who look at the role the Grammy Awards have played for the music industry, and Anand and Jones (2008), analysing the Man Booker Prize's influence on contemporary English-language literature. Murray et al. (2012) draw attention to the networking opportunities provided by the bestowal of awards. The difference between awards and money is discussed in Frey and Gallus (2014) and Gallus and Frey (2016a).

The negative effect of external interventions on intrinsic motivation has first been highlighted in psychology by Deci (1971, 1975) and Deci and Ryan (1985). It has been introduced into economics as 'crowding-out' and 'crowding-in of intrinsic motivation' by Frey (1992, 1997), and is discussed, for instance, in Besley and Ghatak (2005), Bowles (2008, 2009), and Bénabou and Tirole (2003). Extensive empirical evidence is provided in Frey and Jegen (2001) and, with a focus on pro-social behaviour, in Gneezy et al. (2011) and Bowles and Polania-Reyes (2012). Lacetera (2016) offers a useful discussion of the more nuanced recent findings on motivational crowding effects in the context of pro-social behaviour, highlighting the important role of people's perceptions of the incentives in place: It is in particular when incentives are viewed as payments for services rather than as signs of gratitude that they risk undermining pro-social behaviour. For more literature focusing on intrinsic motivation, see, for instance, Mihaly Csikszentmihalyi's (1997) work on *Flow*, Daniel Pink's (2011) book *Drive: The Surprising Truth About What Motivates Us*, and Dan Ariely's (2016) new publication, *Payoff: The Hidden Logic That Shapes Our Motivations*. An ethical perspective on incentives is put forward by Grant (2011).

Economics literature relevant for the analysis of awards can be found in the research on tournaments and contests (Lazear and Rosen 1981), incentive contracts (Baker 1992; Malcomson 2012), non-monetary rewards (Jeffrey 2004), gift-giving (Kube et al. 2012; Non 2012), feedback (Bandiera et al. 2009; Blanes i Vidal and Nossol 2011), recognition (Bradler et al. 2016; Ellingsen and Johannesson 2008; Magnus 1981), identity (Akerlof and Kranton 2000, 2005), reputation systems (Bolton et al. 2013; Resnick et al. 2000), status, positional goods, and rank (Auriol and Renault 2008; Besley and Ghatak 2008; Frank 1985; Scitovsky 1976; Tran and Zeckhauser 2012), and superstars (Koutsobinas 2014; Rosen 1981). The study of awards also builds on the theories of adverse selection (Bannier et al. 2013; Rothschild and Stiglitz 1976) and multitasking (Fehr and Schmidt 2004; Holmström and Milgrom 1991). Aspects of trust, loyalty, appreciation, and esteem are discussed in Brennan and Pettit (2004). Motivations for set completion have been studied, for example, by Carey (2008) and Evers et al. (2016). These and related studies suggest that there is still a lot of potential for interesting research on the design features of awards and their implications for people's motivations and behaviour.

2

Awards are Popular

An alien looking at social life here on earth would be stunned by the enormous number of awards adorning people's chests and organizations' entry halls. They range from orders bequeathed by heads of state, to decorations handed out by the military, and to many different prizes bequeathed by all sorts of organizations in the for-profit and non-profit sectors. Titles, another type of award, are ubiquitous in our world. It is difficult to find an area of society in which honours are not employed.

The Ancient Egyptians valued awards, such as the Order of the Golden Fly for military achievement. Romans used awards in the form of *torcs* (open neck rings), *armilla* (armbands), *phalerae* (disks worn on the breastplate), *corona* (crowns), and *hasta pura* or *hasta donatica* (spears without a head) to decorate distinguished soldiers, and the titles of *pater patriae* or *imperator* in the civil sphere. Historically, the use of awards is intimately related to monarchic systems, with sovereigns first granting membership in orders of chivalry, and later visibly bequeathing the orders' insignia to members of the nobility. Interestingly, in their early days, many orders did not even have such visible insignia, such that only a limited group of insiders knew who belonged to the distinguished circle. While it may seem that honours systems are a backbone of monarchic regimes, we like to point out that even staunch republics have from early on relied on orders to reward merit. Up to this day awards have remained ubiquitous both in monarchies and in republics.

State Orders

The French Republic hands out the highly valued *Légion d'honneur*, which ranges from the *Chevalier* up to the *Grand-Croix*. Napoléon Bonaparte founded it when he was First Consul, and later extended it when he became Emperor. It became a model for many other modern orders of merit, which are often subdivided into similar classes. Italy, for instance, has an *Ordine al Merito della Repubblica Italiana*, whose five grades begin with the *Cavaliere* and range up to the *Cavaliere di Gran Croce*.

German Presidents bequeath the *Bundesverdienstkreuz* (formally called *Verdienstorden der Bundesrepublik Deutschland*, or Order of Merit of the Federal Republic of Germany), which has eight classes. The United States President and Congress bestow several important medals, such as the Congressional Gold Medal, first awarded in 1776, the Presidential Medal of Freedom, created in 1963, and the Presidential Citizens Medal, created in 1969. Communist countries such as the Soviet Union or the German Democratic Republic also handed out medals and titles (such as Hero of the Soviet Union or Hero of Socialist Labour), and they did so in great numbers. Awards, in particular state orders, may also be given to countries and cities. Thus, the George Cross was given to Malta, and the *Légion d'honneur* to sixty-eight cities, among them Algiers, Liège, Belgrade, Luxembourg, and Stalingrad (today Volgograd).

Among the most highly regarded monarchic orders is the Order of the Golden Fleece, founded in 1430 by Philip III, Duke of Burgundy. It can be seen on portraits of kings and emperors, and is worn at formal occasions, for instance by the King of Spain, who is one of its two Grand Masters (besides the Head of the House of Habsburg). Another very old order carries the curious name of Order of the Elephant (*Elefantordenen* in Danish). It has existed in its current form since 1693 and is Denmark's highest and oldest order of knighthood.

Today, the best-known order arguably is the Order of the Garter, which is one of the most cherished orders. It was founded in 1348 and is given as the British Sovereign's personal gift. The United Kingdom has a number of orders (see Table 2.1) ceremonially bequeathed by the Queen.

Table 2.1 UK orders of chivalry and orders of merit, with date of establishment

Order of the Garter (KG)*	1348
Order of the Thistle (KT)*	1687
Order of the Bath (GCB)**	1725
Order of St. Michael and St. George (GCMG)**	1818
Distinguished Service Order (DSO)	1886
Royal Victorian Order (GCVO)**	1896
Order of Merit (OM)	1902
Imperial Service Order (ISO)	1902
Order of the British Empire (GBE)**	1917
Order of the Companions of Honour (CH)	1917

* The letters in parentheses refer to the post-nominal initials used by male recipients, Knights.
** The letters in parentheses stand for Knight Grand Cross.

The honours given on the occasion of the Queen's 90th birthday in June 2016 were the most diverse since the Order of the British Empire was founded in 1917, with the greatest ever number of recipients coming from Black, Asian, or Minority Ethnic backgrounds (Cabinet Office 2016). Almost half of the 1,149 award recipients (538 persons) were women; 5.2 per cent of the successful candidates considered themselves to have a disability under the Equality Act 2010; 1,004 candidates received an Order of the British Empire: 312 received the British Empire Medal (BEM), 477 were appointed a Member of the Order of the British Empire (MBE), and 215 were distinguished as an Officer of the British Empire (OBE); 70 per cent of the recipients had undertaken outstanding work in their communities, either in a voluntary or paid capacity. Among the higher awards, two individuals received a Companion of Honour (CH), one a Knight Grand Cross of the Order of the British Empire (GBE), three a Knight Commander of the Order of the Bath (KCB), thirteen became a Dame Commander of the Order of the British Empire, and nineteen were made a Knight Bachelor (Kt) and are now called 'Sir'. Each year in January, there is a New Year's Honours List with a similar number of recipients.

In most cases, it is the British government which decides who is to be honoured. A particular case is the Resignation Honours. These are granted at the wish of outgoing Prime Ministers following their departure from office. The peerages and other orders can be given to any number of people of their choosing, and some of these lists have attracted criticism in the past. The resignation honours given by Harold Wilson in 1976 created an outright scandal because a number of recipients were wealthy businessmen whose principles were considered antithetic to those held by the Labour Party. Upon his resignation in July 2016, Prime Minister David Cameron presented a list of no fewer than forty-six individuals to receive an order, ranging from a CH (Companion of Honour) and a KCMG (Knight Commander of the Order of St. Michael and St. George), down to sixteen MBEs (Members of the British Empire).

As can be seen in Table 2.1, there are so many orders that for ordinary persons it is not easy to remember what, for instance, KCVO means (the post-nominal letters stand for Knight Commander of the Royal Victorian Order). Interestingly, the public cares little about the ranks within and between orders. But those persons who have received a particular order are well aware of the subtle differences between the various ranks. This may provide an incentive (whether wanted or not) to further climb the ladder of distinction.

Some orders were founded to reward truly extraordinary behaviour. A good example is the Military Order of Maria Theresa, founded in 1757.

It was given to officers who had acted on their own initiative, sometimes even disobeying the commands of higher-ups, but whose behaviour resulted in a successful military act, i.e. winning a battle. In contrast, those who did not follow a command and lost the battle were punished and dismounted. Honouring courage and (a certain degree of) reckless-ness still remains a major function of awards in the military sector. Thus, the advent of drone warfare sparked a fierce debate in the United States, where it was questioned whether drone pilots fighting at a distance merit to be honoured with medals. At the root of this debate lies the question of whether awards should be given for effort and courage, or also for impact (e.g. the number of killings).

The only country among the 196 countries of the world that does not hand out state orders is Switzerland. The reason is that leading Swiss personalities had received orders from foreign countries to induce them to provide mercenaries or other services. In order to stop this practice, since 1848, an article in the Constitution (now it is a law) has forbidden members of the federal government and public officials, members of the army, and judges of the federal courts to accept titles, official presents, and orders. Consequently, there are no Swiss orders. However, this practice is not followed strictly. The Swiss Army gives awards for example to excellent marksmen. Its members are allowed to decorate their uniforms with awards received for peace support and as UN Mili-tary Observers. Also, the twenty-six cantons hand out a considerable number of awards, especially for cultural activities.

Not only monarchs and governments bestow awards. Non-profit organizations hand out a large number of honours, too. In the arts and media, sports, religion, the voluntary sector, and academia, awards are most prominent. Even the for-profit sector, which is supposedly only geared to increasing financial gain, sports an astonishing number and diversity of honours. We will point out and discuss some of them.

Arts, Media, and Fashion

The Academy Awards (Oscars) and the prizes given at film festivals, for example those in Cannes, Venice, Locarno, and Berlin, feature many different categories to recognize personalities in the movie industry. The Emmy Awards honour outstanding achievement in television and the Grammy Awards are given for artistic significance in the field of record-ing in the United States. The prestigious Pulitzer Prize is awarded in no less than twenty-one categories, ranging from Breaking News Reporting to History, Poetry, and Music. There are several major literary prizes handed out in various countries around the globe, such as the famous British Man Booker Prize and France's Prix Goncourt, the German Book Prize, Israel's Jerusalem Prize, Japan's Akutagawa Prize, and of course the Nobel Prize in Literature. Museums and other arts institutions also bestow honours upon their supporters, in particular in the form of titles, such as benefactor or patron. The field of fashion design, engrained in extravagance and media attention, also has a wide range of awards and prizes (e.g. the British Fashion Awards and the ELLE Style Awards). The accompanying red-carpet events provide an important occasion for those deemed influential to see each other and, most importantly, to be seen.

Sports

In regular intervals, the titles Olympic or World Champion, as well as national, regional, and city champions, are awarded. In chess, there are International Masters (IM) and Grandmasters (GM). Athletes get the honour of being elected Sports Personality of the Year and are admitted into one of the many Halls of Fame. In soccer, the FIFA accords Orders of Merit to honour particularly successful players. At world championships, not only is the winning team awarded a golden trophy; specific players are also singled out for their special performance, being made Man of the Match or being given the Golden Ball, Golden Boot, or Golden Glove (all of which are sponsored by private firms).

Religion

Organizations such as the Roman Catholic Church also bestow honours, for instance in the form of titles, such as Canon, Monsignore, or Bishop of some long-disappeared historic diocese. Bishops and Cardinals carry the honorific titles Excellency and Eminence, respectively. Beatifications and canonizations honour distinguished religious persons and can be considered post mortem awards. The rate at which individuals have been elevated to sainthood has greatly risen over the past decades. A recent case in point is Pope Francis' decision to elevate both of his two deceased immediate predecessors, John XXIII and John Paul II, to the honour of a saint.

Voluntary and Humanitarian Sector

Non-profit organizations bequeath many different awards; it is an important way for them to express recognition and gratitude for extraordinary pro-social deeds, and to motivate outsiders to join their ranks. As they abstain from pursuing profits as their goal, paying high salaries to their employees and supporters is often considered to be inconsistent with their purpose (and may also be out of the scope of their budget). Awards are a most suitable way to honour their members, to induce them to uphold their efforts, and to express and make salient the purpose of the organization. It would not come as a surprise if we learned that some non-profits use awards to lure their board members into staying at the very moment when they could otherwise consider moving on to the next organization to extend their networks and gain new experience.

The Florence Nightingale Medal is a widely known award in the voluntary and humanitarian sector. It is given by the International Committee of the Red Cross in order to honour nurses for 'exceptional courage and devotion'. At a more local level, voluntary organizations such as the fire fighters recognize their members' courage and engagement with many different forms of honours, which are mostly based on tenure or courageous deeds in the face of danger. Volunteer fire departments are a prevalent organizational form, and they widely rely on awards as motivators. These awards are given by non-state entities, such as the German Fire Service Association (*Deutscher Feuerwehrverband*), which bestows the German Fire Brigade Honour Cross (*Deutsches Feuerwehr-Ehrenkreuz*), or the Austrian Federal Fire Service Association, which has eight different awards, including a Grand Cross of Merit and a Ring of Honour. Finally, award schemes are also used in service clubs such as Rotary or Lions, which constitute yet another form of organization active in the humanitarian sector.

The types of behaviour that are honoured by voluntary and humanitarian organizations vary. Awards can be given for specific actions, such as donating an organ, for general services, or even for life achievements.

Academia

It might be thought that in higher education and research, as a place of rational interaction, there is little room for symbolic honours and flattery. The opposite is true: academia has an elaborate and extensive system of honours. Universities hand out the titles of honorary doctor or senator, and professional scientific associations award an enormous number of medals and prizes. The best-known ones are certainly the Nobel Prizes and the Fields Medal in mathematics, which many would consider the pinnacle of the academic honour system. Besides awards honouring past achievements, there are early career awards (e.g. the John Bates Clark Medal for economists under 40 in the United States, or the Yrjö Jahnsson Award for European economists under 45) and fellowships celebrating the winners' potential (e.g. what is widely known as the MacArthur Genius grants).

There is an intricate system of titles (not always connected to functions) within universities, such as that of lecturer, reader, assistant professor, associate professor (with and without tenure), full professor, named professor, university professor, distinguished professor, and senior professor. Few academics would probably deny that we attach great importance even to the titles that have no material or monetary implications. In the United States and increasingly also in other regions of the world, universities and student bodies hand out teaching awards—most likely as a counter-balance to the focus on doing research.

Some of the prestigious fellowships given by academies of science allow for the use of post-nominal letters, similar to what we know from state orders. Examples are Fellow of the Royal Society (FRS), founded in 1660; Fellow of the Royal Society of Edinburgh (FRSE), founded among others by Adam Smith in 1783; Fellow of the American Academy of Arts and Sciences, founded in 1780; and, more recently, Fellow of the Academy of the Social Sciences in Australia (FASSA), established in 1971. Finally, there is a flood of best paper awards handed out at conferences and by journals. Academia probably comes close to the state, military, and the arts in terms of the number of awards bestowed.

Business

Most surprising may be the widespread use of awards in the corporate sector, where the only valid currency, after all, is supposed to be money. But titles are very important, even if they are at times only faintly related to functions. Which manager is not, at the very least, a vice-president, or even better, a senior vice-president, or first senior vice-president? The number of titles of Chief Officers has virtually exploded. There is a CEO (Chief Executive Officer), a COO (Chief Operating Officer), a CFO (Chief Financial Officer), a CRO (Chief Risk Officer), a CDO (Chief

Table 2.2 Award types and characteristics

Type	Examples	Characteristics
Honours and distinctions	Trophies, medals, prizes, badges, ribbons, plaques, certificates, honorary titles, orders, crosses, decorations	With or without money or gift Incentive: ex ante (pre-determined criteria) vs ex post Regularity and frequency Confirmatory vs discretionary vs lottery Receipt: expected vs unexpected Decision: peers vs management vs experts Recipients: a) individual vs groups and organizations b) insider vs outsider c) number of winners

Development Officer), a CSO (Chief Strategy Officer), a CIO (Chief Information Officer), and a CVO (Chief Visionary Officer), among many other variants. It seems as though there is a CXO title for every manager, with the X just being filled out by the respective activity. Firms also commend their own employees for being Salesman of the Week or Employee of the Month; the ingenuity to invent ever-new awards seems limitless. The media fervently support and also actively engage in this activity, for instance by regularly choosing the Manager of the Month, the Manager of the Year, the Most Powerful Woman in Business, or even the Manager or Entrepreneur of the Century.

Table 2.2 presents an overview of some examples and characteristics of honours and distinctions. As can be seen, a great many variations are possible and have indeed been used in the field.

Innovation Prizes

Innovation prizes (also referred to as 'inducement prizes') are a special type of award that seeks to promote new ways of overcoming economic and social problems. A monetary sum and public acclaim are promised to that person or group of persons finding a solution to a well-specified problem. A famous example is what today is called the Longitude Prize. The establishment of this prize in 1714 was the British government's response to the scientists' and seafarers' longstanding inability to develop a practicable method for exactly determining a ship's longitude, an important pre-requisite for successful military and commercial navigation in the open seas. While the specialists' greatest hopes were attached to a solution based on astronomy, it was a clockmaker who finally came up with the winning solution: a marine chronometer. Though successful, the clockmaker's unorthodox solution was never officially proclaimed the winning entry (though it did win him several instalments of money).

Another famous example, this one dating from the beginning of the twentieth century, is the Orteig Prize. Raymond Orteig, a New York hotel owner, offered 25,000 US dollars in 1919 (about 340,000 US dollars as of 2014) to the first aviator to fly non-stop across the Atlantic from New York to Paris. Charles Lindbergh won the prize in 1927 and became a national hero. This achievement greatly increased public interest in air travel.

A contemporary example of an innovation prize, named after the first major innovation prize, is the Longitude Prize 2014. This challenge offers a prize fund of 10 million British pounds (roughly 12.5 million euros) to its winners. It has been launched to help solve one of the greatest issues of our time. Which issue exactly the prize would target was decided by members of the British public, who were asked to cast their vote. The target for 2014 became the development of a cost-effective and rapid test to help health professionals select the right antibiotics in time. The prize has been developed and is being run by Nesta, the United Kingdom's innovation foundation, with support from the Technology Strategy Board, the United Kingdom's innovation agency. In the United States, the X Prize Foundation is specialized on innovation prizes, such as the well-known Ansari X Prize offering 10 million US dollars (7.5 million euros, 6 million British pounds) for the first non-governmental team launching a manned spacecraft into space twice within two weeks.

Innovation prizes have a great advantage over research conducted within an organization, say, a ministry or a corporation. They leave open what approach is to be used and what person or persons make an effort to solve the problem. This is strategically valuable because often the winning solution comes from individuals whose technical expertise is far from the field within which the problem originated. It can therefore be beneficial to open the group of potential innovators to outsiders. This can be achieved with innovation prizes.

Ironic and Mock Prizes

Awards are given to honour individuals and organizations for their achievements. They have reached such popularity, however, that it has become fashionable for organizations to create the opposite in order to stand out: awards to shame recipients, or to make fun of them, or to deal with honours themselves with a twinkling eye. There exist a large number of such ironic, mock, and shaming prizes. Let us turn to some of the best-known ones.

Ig Nobel Prize

This award is a parody of the Nobel Prize and its name is based on a pun, combining 'ignoble', i.e. disreputable, with Nobel Prize. The Prize is awarded each year to ten unusual and imaginative achievements in science by the magazine *Annals of Improbable Research*, and it draws considerable media attention. It is usually handed out by genuine Nobel Prize winners, thus also raising the Ig Nobel Prize's prominence. But the Ig Nobel Prize is not only designed to make fun; it also has a more serious intention. According to the prize committee, the Ig Nobel Prize intends to 'honor achievements that first make people laugh, and then make them think'. They are meant to 'spur people's interest in science, medicine, and technology'. Among its notable winners is Sir Andre Geim, who in 2010 received both an Ig Nobel Prize and a Nobel Prize in Physics.

Golden Raspberry Awards

Razzies, as they are often called, are given for the worst performance in film. They are meant to be the opposite of the Academy Awards (Oscars) and are given for 'achievements' in similar categories. For instance, in 2010 the movie *Battlefield Earth* received the prize for the 'Worst Picture of the Decade'. In the same year, Sandra Bullock received the 'Worst Actress' award—and the following night, the Oscar for the 'Best Actress' (yet in another film). Other 'Worst Actress' awardees are Halle Berry, Madonna, and Bo Derek. Paris Hilton received the 'Worst Actress of the Decade' award. Among the 'Worst Actors' are Arnold Schwarzenegger and Sylvester Stallone. Interestingly, some recipients attend the ceremony to collect their prize.

Further Dishonourable and Mock Awards

Bad Sex in Fiction Awards are given by the Literary Review to the author producing the worst description of a sex scene in a novel. A wooden spoon is an award bequeathed to an individual or a team having finished last in a competition. It is mainly given on educational or sporting events. At the Tour de France, the cyclist who finishes last without missing the time cut is accorded the Lanterne Rouge, which sets him apart from other slow racers. The United States Military Academy, also known as West Point, decorates the cadet who finishes last in class by making him the Goat of West Point.

Our discussion shows that awards are commonly used in many different forms and in almost all areas of society. They include formal state orders, distinctions in sport, titles in religion, and further honours in the voluntary sector, academia, and business. Innovation prizes, although they mostly come with a monetary prize purse, certainly also derive part of their incentive effect from the recognition they confer. And even ironic and mock prizes, which probably emerged as a reaction to the many 'normal' honours, can have an important motivating function.

The Academic Study of Honours

The study of orders has evolved into a discipline of its own, called phaleristics (coined after the Roman order, *phalera*). This discipline is historically or legally oriented and concentrates on particular orders, such as the Most Honourable Order of the Bath or the Most Distinguished Order of St. Michael and St. George. Phaleristics focuses to a considerable extent on the collection and the corresponding market of insignia. This literature is not concerned with analysing why a particular person or group received an order, or why somebody received a particular order rather than some other reward. Nor does it study the effects of orders on subsequent performance. This holds also for other fields, such as sociology, whose interest in awards and distinctions has a different focus.

Despite the importance of awards in society, research in social science has largely disregarded them. This neglect applies in particular to economics. Various potential explanations for this disregard can be adduced.

First, according to standard neoclassical economics, the effectiveness of awards as an explicit incentive may be questioned. Awards are mainly symbolic. Although some are accompanied by prize money, there is usually no direct material benefit. Awards are not fungible, i.e. they cannot be used for the purpose the recipient chooses. In contrast, fungible monetary compensation allows the recipient to decide for what purpose to use the revenue. Money can therefore be seen as a superior instrument for inducing effort.

Second, awards may be considered just a reflection of success. Take the example of Richard Branson, the founder of Virgin Airlines, who was knighted for his achievements in air transport. Or Steve Jobs who in 2009 was named CEO of the Decade by *Fortune* magazine for having transformed American business. These achievements were already attained and were likely not induced by expecting the respective honour.

Third, awards as such may be taken to be of little interest to their recipients. After all, awards have little direct material value. The more relevant value of awards could be the increase in future income potentially induced by being better known and having been selected as a good performer. There is certainly some truth to this. It has been empirically shown, for instance, that academics can profit from being awarded a major book prize (e.g. the Pulitzer Prize, or the Financial Times or Goldman Sachs Business Book of the Year Awards): they can capitalize on such awards by demanding higher fees on the speakers' market (Chan et al. 2014). Awards may also improve the health of their recipients. It has been calculated that, on average, scholars who had received the Nobel Prize in Physics or Chemistry between 1901 and 1950 lived between one and two years longer than non-winning nominees (Rablen and Oswald 2008). Similarly, it has been found that Oscar winning actors on average lived about four years longer than actors who were otherwise comparable but did not win the award (Redelmeier and Singh 2001a, 2001b). It has also been shown that literary awards, such as the Italian Strega Prize, have greatly increased the winners' book sales (Ponzo and Scoppa 2015).

Recipients of the Nobel Prize certainly value the honour over and above the accompanying or subsequent monetary reward or improvement in health. Quite generally, awards are highly coveted even with no money attached. Several studies indicate that people do indeed value status independently of the monetary consequence; they are willing to incur material costs to improve their status and rank (e.g. see Huberman et al. 2004; Tran and Zeckhauser 2012). As awards are important producers of status, it should be expected that people attach intrinsic value to them. They are likely to invest much effort and money to be able to showcase particular awards. For example, in the case of the Order of Leopold, which is bequeathed in Belgium, the insignia going with the honour must be purchased—and recipients seem happy to do so.

Conversely, some prizes, medals, and awards that are accompanied by large sums of money are nevertheless relatively unknown within the relevant community, say, academia. A case in point is the scientific Balzan Prize, which gives no less than 1 million Swiss Francs to the winner; and yet, few scholars seem to be aware of it.

While economists have largely neglected the study of awards, several individuals have made noteworthy contributions. Weisbrod and

Hansen (1972) made an 'effort to provide a building block for a "general theory of awards"'(p. 422). However, their lead was not taken up until recently (Besley 2005; Frey 2005, 2007). There have since been several empirical analyses on which we draw in our book. Table 2.3 presents a survey of various contributions.

Table 2.3 shows that the study of awards now covers many different areas, including business, academia, culture, publishing, and voluntary public good contributions. Many of these first empirical studies find that awards can have significant positive motivational effects.

Our book intends to make the point that awards merit careful consideration. This is especially important in times where obsession about payment schemes and ever-increasing bonuses risks focusing our attention too much on financial values at the expense of honours and symbolic distinction for meritorious acts. Awards, which derive their value from honour and esteem, may serve as a valuable corrective. They open a new field of research that is intrinsically fascinating. We show the many aspects involved in award bestowals, and by doing so we hope to open the perspective of economists and others interested in human motivation and incentives for this fascinating field.

Conclusions

Awards, mostly in the form of orders, decorations, and crosses, have historically played a large role in monarchies as well as in republics. Today, awards are widely used in most if not all areas of society. State orders exist in great variety and they are typically further subdivided into several different classes. The fields of arts, media, fashion, and sports also have a large number of awards. Quality cannot be easily inferred in the cultural sphere, which might explain the importance of awards as signals of quality in the former three fields. Yet, even in sports, where performance is clearly visible in the outcome of the game, awards and prizes play a prominent role.

Religious organizations as well as organizations in the voluntary and humanitarian sector also rely heavily on the use of awards. In this case, the importance of awards can be explained by the fact that intrinsic, non-monetary (and even other-worldly) motivations are crucial in these fields. Moreover, non-profit organizations in the humanitarian sector are frequently cash-constrained, and awards offer a relatively inexpensive way of motivating members to continue their engagement. At the same time, awards make this engagement public and may hence induce others to emulate the award recipients' behaviour.

Table 2.3 Empirical literature on awards and the effects found

Field	Performance Dimension	Authors	Award	Research Design	Result
Society	General	Frey (2006)	Honours, state orders	Analytic narratives	Awards are more efficient where performance is ambiguous
Business	Attendance	Markham et al. (2002)	Attendance award programme, ex ante, symbolic	Quasi-experiment, manufacturing plants	Increase in attendance (absenteeism lowered by 29%–52%)
		Gubler et al. (2016)	Attendance award programme, ex ante, lottery, gift certificate	Quasi-experiment, laundry plant	Gaming, crowding-out, reducing plant productivity by 1.4%
	Voluntary work behaviours	Neckermann et al. (2014)	Award for social activities, ex post, certificate & bonus	Panel data analysis	Positive spillover, raising core task performance by 7.4%, short-lived
	Knowledge sharing	Neckermann and Frey (2013)	Hypothetical award, ex ante	Survey experiment, IBM	Increase in stated willingness to share knowledge
	Sales (software)	Larkin (2011)	Entry into Sales Club, ex ante, symbolic & luxury trip	Field data, regression discontinuity	Award is valued at $27,000 by average salesperson
	Management, leadership	Wade et al. (2006)	CEO of the Year medals	Event study	Positive abnormal stock returns in short term, negative long-term impact
		Malmendier and Tate (2009)	CEO business press awards	Field data, matching	Negative effect on firm performance, CEOs turn to outside activities
Business/State		Siming (2016)	Swedish orders of merit	Natural experiment, diff-in-diff	Orders substitute for part of CEOs' monetary compensation
	Innovation	Brunt et al. (2012)	Innovation awards, Royal Agricultural Society of England	Analysis of data on prize competitions	Increase in competition, medals more important than monetary awards
		Moser and Nicholas (2013)	Innovation awards, Crystal Palace Exhibition	Analysis of US patent data	Prizes encourage future innovation (40% increase in patenting)
	Data entry	Kosfeld and Neckermann (2011)	Congratulatory card, ex ante	Experiment with students	Increase in performance by 12%
Lab	Rent-seeking game	Huberman et al. (2004)	'Winner' tag, applause, ex ante	Laboratory experiment	People are willing to forgo material gain to attain public recognition

Category	Subcategory	Study	Award	Method	Findings
Science	Knowledge production	Chan et al. (2014)	John Bates Clark Medal	Synthetic control method	Increase in publications & citations (13% & 50% after five years), long-lasting
			Econometric Society Fellowship	Synthetic control method	Increase in publications & citations (15% & 37% after five years), long-lasting
		Borjas and Doran (2015)	Fields Medal	Comparing winners with contenders	Decline in winners' productivity (publications, citations, students mentored)
Public good	Knowledge production	Gallus (2016)	Award given by committee of editors, ex post, symbolic	Field experiment, German Wikipedia	Increase in newcomer retention rate by 20%
		Restivo and van de Rijt (2012)	Informal peer-to-peer reward given by another editor, ex post, symbolic	Field experiment, English Wikipedia	Increase in most prolific editors' productivity by 60%
	Blood donation	Lacetera and Macis (2010)	Medal for meeting blood donation quotas, ex ante	Longitudinal data analysis	Increase in frequency of blood donations
Public health	Performance on test	Ashraf et al. (2014)	Congratulatory letter, mention in newsletter, ex ante	Field experiment, Zambia	Zero net effect
	Condom sales	Ashraf et al. (2014)	Stars on display in shop, ex ante	Field experiment, Zambia	Higher increase in effort for non-financial rewards than financial rewards
Arts & culture	General	Ginsburgh and van Ours (2003)	Oscars, Man Booker Prize, other awards in the arts	Comparing winners with contenders	Positive influence of awards on winners' performance
		Kovács and Sharkey (2014)	Prestigious book awards	Comparing winners with contenders	Less favourable quality evaluations for winners

Notes: 'ex ante' and 'ex post' in the Award column indicate whether the award is an explicitly announced ex ante incentive, or whether it is given ex post.

Source: Jana Gallus and Bruno S. Frey (2016a). 'Awards: A strategic management perspective'. *Strategic Management Journal* 37(8): 1699–714.

Academia and the business sector exhibit an uncountable number of awards. They are also characterized by an elaborate system of titles. Awards can even be found at the intersection of the two fields, for instance when honorary doctorates are given to business people, or when researchers accept distinctions from the business press.

Innovation prizes, or 'inducement prizes', are a special type of award. By offering a monetary prize to the person or group finding a solution to a well-defined problem, the givers of innovation prizes seek to incite research into important economic and social challenges while leaving the methods and approach of problem solving open.

The study of awards has for a long time been largely neglected by the social sciences, in particular economics, while monetary incentives have received considerable attention. Our book seeks to redress this imbalance.

Related Literature

A (necessarily incomplete) list of different types of official awards can be found in the Wikipedia entry, 'List of Prizes, Medals, and Awards' (https://en.wikipedia.org/wiki/List_of_prizes,_medals_and_awards). See also Robertson (2010) and, for the United Kingdom, the report by the House of Commons (2004).

For detailed accounts of single state orders, see, for example, Risk (1972) on the Most Honourable Order of the Bath, or Galloway (2002) on the Order of St. Michael and St. George.

Best (2008, 2011) gives a useful overview of prizes to illustrate their abundance, while also providing further references to literature. A discussion of prizes in the cultural sector can be found in Levy (1987), Holden (1994), and Nelson et al. (2001), all focusing on the Academy Awards, or more generally in Ginsburgh and van Ours (2003), Ginsburgh and Weyers (2014), and English (2005, 2014). Ponzo and Scoppa (2015) discuss the effect of receiving the Italian Strega Prize on the respective subsequent book sales, and Kovács and Sharkey (2014) point to the potential negative effects of book prizes on readers' ratings.

On awards in sports, Allen and Parsons (2006), for instance, analyse the determinants of induction into the Baseball Hall of Fame. In an analysis of the emotional reactions of bronze and silver medallists at the 1992 Summer Olympics, Medvec et al. (1995) find that bronze medallists tend to be happier than silver medallists; a result that the authors attribute to the fact that the most compelling counterfactual alternative for the silver medallist was winning gold, whereas for the bronze medallist it was going home without any medal at all. For

religious honours, Barro et al. (2011) study the Catholic Church's practice of beatification and canonization. Delmonico et al. (2002) present
specific awards in the humanitarian sector. For a discussion of honours
in academia, see, for example, Zuckerman (1992).

The abundance of prizes bequeathed by corporations is documented
in Tise (2014). Titles and awards in the business sector are analysed by
Wade et al. (2006), Malmendier and Tate (2009), and Ammann et al.
(2016), who look at awards given to CEOs, such as the title Manager of
the Year. Jeffrey (2004) and Neckermann et al. (2014) discuss the benefits of tangible, non-monetary incentives for employees and provide
arguments why they may accomplish a firm's employee motivation
goals better than cash incentives of equal market value.

The fact that awards provide their recipients with future monetary
benefits is shown in several studies looking at different fields. In one of
our studies in the field of academia (Chan et al. 2014), we empirically
show that academics can profit from being awarded a major book prize
because they may subsequently demand higher speaking fees for the
talks they give outside the field of academia (e.g. at events in the private
sector).

The discussion of innovation prizes draws on the interesting work by
Jeppesen and Lakhani (2010), who show empirically that the winners of
science problem-solving contests are often people whose field of technical expertise is distant from the field in which the problem originated.
Prestigious non-pecuniary awards have been documented to be potentially even more effective in fostering competitive entry into innovation
contests than are monetary rewards. Analysing one of the longest available datasets of awards for innovation, offered by the Royal Agricultural
Society of England in the nineteenth and twentieth centuries, Brunt
et al. (2012) conclude that 'medals were more important than monetary
awards' (p. 657) in encouraging competition and innovation. See also
Moser and Nicholas (2013) for an analysis of non-monetary awards as
an instrument to encourage innovation.

The detailed story of the Longitude Prize is recounted in Sobel (1995).
As the author describes, the clockmaker John Harrison, who unexpect-
edly brought up the unorthodox winning solution, had great difficulties
in collecting his prize. In fact, he was never officially recognized as the
winner.

The assumption that people value awards even if they confer no
material or career-related advantage is supported by the field experiment
in Gallus (2016). Similar positive effects of awards as a valued resource are
found in Ammann et al. (2016), Siming (2016), Neckermann et al. (2014),
Neckermann and Frey (2013), Larkin (2011), Kosfeld and Neckermann

(2011), Malmendier and Tate (2009), Wade et al. (2006), and Brennan and Pettit (2004). Huberman et al. (2004), for instance, experimentally show that status is in itself a valued resource. Frank (1985) adduces numerous fascinating examples illustrating the widespread phenomenon of status striving. Lindenberg shows in various theoretical and empirical studies that status is a real social need, in that it helps humans attain social approval (e.g. Lindenberg 1996, 2013). Further studies document that people are willing to incur substantial costs in order to improve their status or rank (Tran and Zeckhauser 2012).

3

Types of Awards

Individuals or Groups Receiving an Award

Honours are given to individuals as well as to groups of individuals, including to organizations as a whole, such as the Red Cross or Médecins Sans Frontières. Individuals are honoured for a performance or for an attitude the donor values, and for going 'beyond the call of duty'.

When a group is honoured, it is sometimes unclear who should be entitled to represent it. When the European Union received the Nobel Peace Prize in 2012, it was rather amusing to note the problems the EU bureaucratic apparatus seemed to have to determine who would attend the Nobel ceremony. After much manoeuvring it was decided that no less than three presidents should act as the actual recipients: the President of the Commission (José Manuel Barroso), the President of the Council of Ministers (Herman Van Rompuy), and the President of the European Parliament (Martin Schulz).

Confirmatory and Discretionary Awards

Two basic types of awards may be distinguished, which have different implications for their givers, winners, and potential winners.

Confirmatory Awards

The first type of award may be called confirmatory awards. These are more or less automatically given, based on clearly defined and observable criteria of achievement, or due to the specific position the person occupies. An exception is only made if the person is considered unfit because of inadequate conduct. The eligibility criteria are fixed and therefore this type of award becomes an ex ante incentive whose receipt can be expected. In many regards this type of award corresponds to the incentives as usually studied by economists. In many countries, confirmatory awards are common practice in the diplomatic and military service as well as among statesmen, other politicians, and top public service officials. High British diplomats, in particular the ambassadors to strategically important countries, normally are honoured with the Order of St. Michael and St. George. Scholars from Commonwealth countries winning the Nobel Prize are appointed Knight Bachelor. Both orders go with the title Sir or Dame, followed by the recipient's first name.

Similarly, when a sportsperson from the Commonwealth wins Olympic gold, he or she can expect to subsequently be appointed a Member of the Order of the British Empire. The recipient can then put the acronym MBE behind his or her name. As our interview with the former President of the Federal Republic of Germany, Professor Roman Herzog, made clear, German sportspersons who have won an Olympic medal automatically receive the Silver Laurel Leaf (*Silbernes Lorbeerblatt*). Only in very rare cases does the President deny this honour, as Roman Herzog did when the would-be prize winner was known to have spied on colleagues during the times of the German Democratic Republic.

In European football, the player with the highest goal score in league matches in a given season automatically receives the Golden Shoe (whereby only the highest league of every UEFA member country is considered and a weighting is applied to take into account the quality of the respective league).

Confirmatory awards are similar to bonus pay. In both cases the rewards are handed out when specific criteria that have been fixed in advance are reached or surpassed. Potential recipients could in principle even go to court if they did indeed meet the criteria but the reward was withheld. In the case of awards the benefit consists in a symbolic order, decoration, or some other form of prize; in the case of bonuses it consists in money. In firms, confirmatory awards are often given in addition to bonus payments, for instance to the salesperson leading the rankings in one of several different dimensions (e.g. life insurance, health insurance, and liability insurance). In this case, the award serves to increase the visibility of top performers, and to increase the salience of the existing ranking hierarchy.

Confirmatory awards bear the risk of inviting strategic action because it is clear what criteria have to be met to win the award. Moreover, zero-sum (or even negative-sum) rat races risk being induced. Agents have an incentive to concentrate all their efforts on meeting or surpassing the criteria while disregarding other aspects of the job. They may even be induced to fake their performance and to manipulate the criteria in their favour. Awards share these problems with monetary bonuses, which are also based on well-defined and measurable criteria.

Discretionary Awards

The second type of award is based on the discretion of the givers. The latter enjoy leeway in decision-making as to whether and to whom to bequeath an award. Indeed, it is one of the few areas in which the actions by decision-makers cannot (or can hardly) be brought to court. It is, for instance, unthinkable that anyone would go to court in order to be made a Knight of the Order of the Garter, or to receive the Nobel Prize. In effect, such a step would defeat the very essence of the award, esteem and honour, which has to be freely granted and cannot be enforced.

Donors have a strong incentive to honour individuals and groups in line with their political, economic, or social interests. However, an award only becomes and remains valuable if it enjoys high prestige. The donors would be ill advised to only consider their short-run and direct interests. Rather, they must balance the benefits received from the award recipients (for instance, a higher productivity at work or political support) with the need to honour individuals and groups generally recognized for their meritorious behaviour.

As discretionary awards depend on the more or less free choice of the giver, there is also scope for pressure activities. These influence activities may well be greater than in the case of confirmatory awards because there is more room for influencing the donor, as the latter is not constrained by transparent criteria.

Many of the empirical analyses covered in this book focus on discretionary awards, because they provide an opportunity to the givers to recognize truly exceptional behaviour, going beyond what is expected or asked for. This type of award acknowledges laudable behaviour ex post and is not a reward individuals normally expect to receive. Discretionary awards allow the givers to respond to the unexpected, and thus possibly induce more of that behaviour on the part of third parties. In contrast, confirmatory awards may be considered part of administrative decision-making where the regulatory framework is supposed to be strictly followed, though in reality this is not always precisely the case. Discretionary awards are clearly different from bonuses, and are therefore worth being studied separately.

In our numerous discussions with people from academia, the non-profit sector, the state, and the business sector, we have repeatedly heard about the demand for clear-cut and well-observable criteria when giving awards. This demand seems to stem from a considerable scepticism or outright fear of according decision-makers discretionary room in their choice of whom to award. The recourse to numbers and formulae to legitimize the bestowal of awards is the natural response. By limiting themselves to confirmatory awards, however, decision-makers in the private, public, and non-profit sectors risk forgoing important opportunities that discretionary awards offer for motivating workers.

Differentiating the Effects of Different Award Characteristics

A Vignette Survey Experiment

In order to get insights into how these motivational effects work, a survey experiment using vignettes was conducted online with the employees of an IBM Research Laboratory (Neckermann and Frey 2013). The survey focused on the effect of introducing an award for voluntary work behaviours, and the paper analyses which award characteristics determine the size of the effect.

A short description of hypothetical scenarios called vignettes was presented to the subjects. They were then asked to indicate their behaviour in case of the described situation. Each situation consisted in randomly selected values for each vignette dimension. The systematic variation of the values in the different dimensions made it possible to estimate the effects of changes in combinations of variables as well as changes in individual variables. Each individual responded to a number of different vignettes so that individual fixed effects could be estimated. In contrast, traditional survey approaches risk eliciting unreliable and biased self-reports, as the questions often are too abstract (see Bertrand and Mullainathan 2001). The vignette technique closely resembles real-life decision-making situations. In particular, respondents evaluate a complete situation describing a bundle of different factors rather than having to state how they think isolated factors will influence their behaviour.

Each vignette described the introduction of a new incentive for all employees at the IBM Research Laboratory. Each subject was randomly assigned a hypothetical award with a particular set of factor levels. The four factors chosen had been considered to be important by all managers, and they varied most between the different awards surveyed.

Factors Determining the Behaviour of Award Recipients

TYPE OF REWARD TO ACCOMPANY THE AWARD

Two types of rewards were considered: cash and gifts of equal monetary value. According to standard economic theory, compensation should be in cash, as this is the most efficient means of compensation due to its fungibility and option value. Consequently, a gift of the same monetary value should not lead to a higher utility than the equivalent payment in cash, which makes gifts inferior incentives. However, motivational crowding and signalling theory (these theories are more fully covered in Chapters 6 and 7) argue that gifts can lead to a higher motivation because gifts are less likely to be perceived as controlling or as destroying the signalling value of certain actions. Social and cognitive psychology describe further advantages of gifts, long neglected in economics, that may be sufficient to reduce or eliminate any inherent advantage of cash as an incentive (Jeffrey and Shaffer 2007). Examples include the social reinforcement associated with the greater visibility of tangible gifts as compared to monetary rewards, and the perceived value of gifts, which may well exceed their monetary value due to the emotional reactions often triggered by gifts.

AMOUNT OF CASH OR VALUE OF GIFT

The accompanying cash payment or gift of the rewards described in the vignettes varied in value between $0 and $10,000. The set of possible values was $0, $50, $150, $300, $1,000, $2,000, $4,000, $6,000, $8,000, and $10,000. For the gifts, four categories were used: zero value, small (about $150), medium (about $2,000), and high value (about $8,000).

DEGREE OF PUBLICITY

Rewards can send signals to outsiders about the recipients' ability and motivation, conferring social recognition among their peers. This, of course, requires that the rewards be made public. To measure the behavioural impact of visibility, each vignette contained one of the following three types of publicity: The list of recipients would either remain undisclosed, or it would be published on the intranet, or it would be published on the intranet and presented at a ceremony.

THE MAXIMUM NUMBER OF RECIPIENTS

The perceived value of an award crucially depends on the award being scarce (e.g. Hirsch 1976). To study the impact of award exclusivity on motivation, the vignette varied the maximum number of award recipients per year. It could be 1, 2, 6, 10, 16, or 20.

The subjects of the survey answered to a number of different situational descriptions. The effect of the award characteristics on these responses was evaluated using a multiple-regression analysis.

Example of a Particular Award Vignette

IBM introduces a new *Cooperation Award*. Nominations must originate within the team and be supported by the project leader or manager. One level of management in the home office needs to approve the award for the nominated person. In recognition of the recipient's contribution, the award comes with a ballpoint pen labelled 'Thank you for your exceptional contribution!'

This represents the first factor referring to the type of accompanying reward. The second factor states that the award recipients would be showcased on the intranet. The other factors are captured by stating that it is a gift of $0. 'There will be up to 16 recipients (about 6% of researchers and non-technical staff) per year in this lab. The lab director congratulates the winner(s) in the presence of the other members of the lab.'

Willingness to Share Research Findings

The subjects were asked to indicate their willingness to share an important research result with their team before publishing it under their own name. Individuals were told that sharing the finding would increase the quality and speed of the team project, but it would also expose them to the personal risk that the finding could be used and published without giving them the appropriate personal credit for the discovery. Alternatively, they could wait and publish the finding in a scientific journal under their own name before sharing it with team colleagues. Hence, individuals acting in the interest of the company would share, whereas those caring more about their private benefit would wait and share later. Respondents marked their willingness on a 10-point scale ranging from 1 = 'I definitely would not share now' to 10 = 'I would certainly share now'.

The vignette was introduced in the following way. First, respondents were asked to state their willingness to share the finding, assuming they were working in their current work environment (status quo). Then, subjects were sequentially confronted with four vignettes, i.e. the scenarios describing the introduction of an award, and asked to indicate their willingness to share the finding in each of them. After the fourth vignette, subjects were randomly asked to imagine that they either did or did not receive the award. They were then asked again about their willingness to share the finding. The survey ended with a section in which respondents were asked questions about personal characteristics, their perception of the role of awards in organizations, and the determinants of award effectiveness in motivating employees.

Fifty-four researchers completed the questionnaire (a response rate of 31 per cent), resulting in 211 observations. The respondents were representative of the workforce with respect to criteria such as age, gender, and length of employment at IBM.

Results

The average willingness to share important information with colleagues after an award was announced in the vignette was 7.31, with a standard deviation of 2.67 on a 10-point scale. The majority of subjects marked a willingness to share between 7 and 10. The analysis in Neckermann and Frey (2013) suggests that the monetary value of the reward had a robust and statistically significant positive impact on the willingness to share a finding. An increase in the value of the award from $0 to $150 increased the stated willingness to share by 0.35. An increase from $0 to $2,000 increased it by 0.52; an increase from $0 to $8,000 increased the stated willingness by 0.62 in the 10-point scale. Zero and small monetary values did not have a statistically significant impact on the stated willingness to share information.

In the qualitative survey conducted after the vignette study, the responding employees confirmed the importance of the monetary prize. Almost all indicated that they considered it to be essential for an award to be accompanied by a substantial monetary bonus. This can be interpreted in different ways. First, the money that comes with the award and not the award per se motivates employees. Second, it is the award per se that motivates employees, but the appreciation of an award depends on whether the award is costly for the employer. Awards that involve costs for the employer ensure that they are meant seriously and that they are not merely used as cheap incentives. Third, employees care about the award but they also care about extra income. Lastly, employees may mispredict the joy or utility they would derive from a symbolic award that is presented in a serious manner to convey public recognition.

Both forms of publicity, announcements of the winners on the intranet and ceremonies, had a positive effect on stated contributions to the public good (i.e. on the willingness to share an idea). Compared to a situation with no publicity, stated contributions were on average 0.49 points higher when the vignette included a ceremony. Naming the recipients and having a ceremony increased stated contributions by as much as increasing the value of the award from $0 to about $1,000. Almost all respondents agreed that awards are important as signals of one's qualities to other employees and outsiders. The coefficient of having a ceremony and announcing the winners on the intranet was larger than the coefficient of an announcement on the intranet alone. For the awards to serve as signals, only the announcement was necessary. While this difference was not statistically significant at the conventional levels, the larger coefficient on the combination of intranet and ceremony suggests that employees may have valued the ceremony per se.

For a given monetary value, gifts seem to work less well than payments in cash. Holding the value of the reward constant, a gift led to a willingness to share that was 0.40 points lower than the willingness induced by an equivalent cash payment. The size of this effect was substantial. It corresponded to an increase of the monetary value from $0 to $300. A substantial number of respondents stated that they preferred money or paid vacation to other kinds of prizes.

The number of recipients did not have a statistically significant effect. Similarly, the demographic variables, such as age, gender, and experience with international teams, did not play any role.

The analysis in Neckermann and Frey (2013) suggests that awards may have significant and systematic effects on employees' stated contributions in a public good situation at work. Stated contributions strictly increased with the monetary value of the reward. Gifts were valued less than their cash equivalent. Publicity mattered greatly. The fact that ceremonies seemed to have a larger impact than a publication on the intranet suggests that recipients may value direct personal recognition.

Demand for Awards

Most people seem to be extremely flattered when receiving awards and recognition in general. We want to discuss four main reasons that we consider to be relevant.

First, awards convey appreciation and recognition. The demand for social recognition and esteem seems deeply ingrained in human behaviour. Social recognition raises our self-evaluation and gives us the feeling that our activity is valuable and indeed valued by others. The higher the giver's prestige, the more actual and hopeful winners may cherish a given award. When asked, many people state that they do not care about being honoured because, so they say, they 'just do their duty'.

However, it can frequently be observed that the same individuals are highly pleased when they, and the activity they engage in, nevertheless are honoured and celebrated in a public ceremony.

Second, awards establish a special relationship between the recipient and the donor. The resulting bond of loyalty holds for both parties. Individuals deciding to accept an award are expected by the giver and by the general public to hold a positive attitude towards the award giver. At the same time, by handing out an award, the giver is expected to maintain a supportive attitude towards the recipient. If these expectations of loyalty are violated, both parties experience a loss of appreciation and the award signal's credibility suffers.

Third, awards often entail social and material advantages. They are sometimes directly accompanied by money or annuities. For instance, an undivided Nobel Prize presently goes with 8 million Swedish kronor (about 683,000 British pounds, or 860,000 euros). Awards may also raise the prospect of a more successful career and higher future income. Young recipients may expect to gain more prominence compared to their competitors, as awards help them gain visibility, which may lead to more prestigious and better-paid positions. However, many awards are not accompanied by money, as is the case with most state orders. We argue that even awards that do not provide any material and/or career-related benefits can have powerful motivational effects. Chapter 5 provides results from a field experiment on purely symbolic awards, which support this conjecture.

Fourth, award recipients gain social status. They enjoy the public recognition and elation, setting them apart from other people. This is also the case with other rewards, such as getting a higher bonus than one's co-workers or peers. However, bonuses are privately given. In many cases the recipients are prohibited to reveal the amount received to other persons, in particular to co-workers. In contrast, awards are invariably given in a public ceremony by one's superior, or even the CEO in person. Awards thus have the added benefit of making the distinction visible to one's reference group, and even beyond (e.g. family and friends).

The demand for honours seems to be almost limitless; there hardly appear to be decreasing returns to receiving prestigious awards. A striking example is the first Duke of Wellington, Arthur Wellesley, who received an almost uncountable number of titles of nobility and military ranks, as well as most of the major orders of his time, as illustrated in Box 3.1.

Somewhat more recently, people remember the chests full of orders and medals of the vain Reichsmarschall Göring, or of the Soviet marshal

---

Box 3.1 SELECTION OF THE TITLES OF NOBILITY, MILITARY RANKS, AND MAJOR ORDERS RECEIVED BY ARTHUR WELLESLEY (1769–1852)

In addition to being the first Duke of Wellington, he was also made Baron and Marquess Douro, Viscount, Earl, and Marquess of Wellington, as well as Conde de Vimeiro, Duque de Vitória, and Marqués de Torres Vedras in Portugal, Ducado de Ciudad Rodrigo in Spain, and Prins van Waterloo in the Netherlands. Wellington was made Knight of the Order of the Garter, Knight of the Most Illustrious Order of the Golden Fleece, Knight Grand Cross of the Order of the Bath, of the Royal Guelphic Order, of the Order of the Sword, of the Orders of the Black Eagle and of the Red Eagle, of the Imperial Military Order of Max Joseph, of the Imperial Military Order of Maria Theresa, and Knight of the Order of the Elephant, as well as Field Marshal of Her Majesty's Forces, of the Austrian Army, of the Hanoverian Army, of the Netherlands, of the Portuguese Army, of the Prussian Army, of the Russian Army, and Captain General of the Spanish Army, among other distinctions.

Box 3.2 DECORATIONS CARRIED BY US GENERAL DAVID HOWELL PETRAEUS

Combat Action Badge, Defence Distinguished Service Medal, Army Distinguished Service Medal, Defence Superior Service Medal, Legion of Merit, Bronze Star, Meritorious Service Medal, Army Commendation, Joint Service Achievement Medal, Humanitarian Service Medal, Army Service Ribbon, Air Assault Badge, Master Parachutist, Joint Meritorious Unit Award, Army Meritorious Unit Commendation, Army Superior Unit Award, besides various other awards.

Zhukov. Sometimes the chests of these persons appear too small to provide enough space for all their awards. But this is not only true for military personnel in dictatorial countries. The famous US four-star General David Petraeus also carried more than twenty decorations on his uniform (Box 3.2).

These examples may already illustrate that awards are not merely a remnant of the past, but that they remain highly desired up to this day. This also holds for the corporate sector and for academia. We would even argue that honours often are of higher value to their recipients than are monetary rewards, in particular for individuals with a decent monetary income. Receiving ever more money loses its appeal due to the decreasing marginal utility of money, a fact well established in the empirical research on happiness (see, e.g., Frey and Stutzer 2002a, 2002b). For individuals with higher incomes, honours become an especially attractive way of gaining social recognition.

Conclusions

Awards are given to individuals, groups, and organizations. They may even be given to objects (e.g. products) and ideas or movements instead of identifiable groups of individuals. The recipients can often be understood as representatives of a larger group, thus spreading the reach of the award.

Two basic types of awards are identified. Confirmatory awards are almost automatically given based on a clearly defined and observable set of eligibility criteria, or due to a particular position the person occupies. Potential risks, such as strategic manipulation and rat races, have to be considered. Discretionary awards, which this book focuses on, grant the giver leeway in deciding whether and to whom to bequeath an award. Such awards serve as a special signal of recognition and allow the giver to respond to the unexpected.

An empirical analysis undertaken in a major corporate research institution suggests that awards can have a significant effect on employees' willingness to contribute to the general goals of their enterprise. The monetary value of awards is considered to be more important than that of a corresponding gift. The publicity going with the award ceremony is taken to be even more significant.

Four major reasons may account for a high and widespread demand for awards. Awards convey appreciation and recognition, they establish a special relationship to the donor, they often enable future social and material advantages, and they provide social status. They also signal to the recipients themselves that they are good at what they are doing.

Stated preferences of potential award recipients, namely that they would not attach any value to public distinction, need not correspond to their true (and at times clearly revealed) preferences. This is illustrated by most people's joy and fondness once they have received an award. As the famous composer and pianist Johannes Brahms (1833–97) aptly put it, 'Orden sind mir wurscht, aber haben will ich sie' ('I don't care about orders, but I do want to have them').

Related Literature

The discussion of the vignette survey study at IBM in Switzerland closely follows Neckermann and Frey (2013). For the methodological approach see, e.g., Rossi and Anderson (1982), McFadden (2001), and Hensher and Johnson (1981).

The distinction between confirmatory and discretionary awards was first introduced in Gallus and Frey (2017). Bruni (2013) also draws attention to the difference between ex ante rewards, or incentives as studied by economists, and awards given ex post for virtuous behaviours (similarly, see Lepper et al. 1973). Our observation that people tend to demand clear and well-observable criteria to legitimize award bestowals finds support in the works by Gerd Gigerenzer. He takes a clear stance in favour of following leaders' intuition, and shows how the recourse to numbers and rankings for fear of being held responsible ('defensive decision-making') can harm organizations (e.g. Gigerenzer 2014).

The awards specifically mentioned in this chapter have been the topic of various publications. More information on the Nobel Prizes can be found in Crawford (1987), Zuckerman (1996), Feldman (2001), and Chan and Torgler (2012). The official website for the Nobel Prizes (nobelprize. org) presents further useful and interesting facts. It also links to a nomination archive, disclosing the lists of nominees for three Nobel Prizes, Physiology or Medicine (1901–51), Literature (1901–50), and Peace (1901–56).

The British Order of St. Michael and St. George, the Knight Bachelor, the Order of the British Empire, and the Order of the Garter are covered in Duckers (2004). Based on archival documents, Tripnaux (2008) provides detailed information on the history and foundation of the Belgian Order of Leopold, whose members have to purchase the insignia in times of peace. The International Balzan Foundation (2012) presents an overview of the Balzan Prize winners' research projects.

For an overview of the honours received by Arthur Wellesley, first Duke of Wellington, including illustrations of some of his orders and decorations, see Stocqueler (1853, pp. 306–14). *The Telegraph* (2010) and Singer-Vine (2011) offer a guide for interpreting the manifold batches and decorations displayed on the uniform of General David Petraeus.

4

Awards and Academic Performance

Awards Honouring or Inducing Best Behaviour?

Awards are given for outstanding achievements. The award givers formally distinguish recipients from other individuals who in their view have performed somewhat less well. At the same time, awards are bequeathed to motivate the recipients to keep on doing excellent work, or possibly to perform even better. This motivation may extend to other persons who aspire to receive an award in the future.

Bequeathing awards may be seen to involve two separate causal relationships. The first is going from high performance to receipt of the award; the second is going from receiving the award to high performance. Both may exist at the same time. Just observing a person being honoured, and performing well, does not allow us to distinguish between the two causal links. The best person wins the award, and the awardee performs best. In this chapter and Chapter 5 we make an effort to separate the two effects. We wish to know whether an award further raises the performance of its recipients in the future. The question is whether honouring people raises their subsequent performance. Such an effect may occur because the motivation of the recipients is bolstered (e.g. due to self-confidence or to an implicitly perceived obligation to live up to others' expectations). A quite different reason may be due to the Matthew effect, meaning that the successful award winners enjoy an elevated status and therefore get better access to resources, which in turn may facilitate higher performance.

The motivational consequences of monetary rewards have been studied extensively (see Chapter 1). It is a basic premise in economics that the more money a person is promised in return for performance, the more he or she is induced to work. This idea also lies behind the movement for variable performance pay, which is widely applied in the corporate sector and consists in adding bonuses to the basic salary.

Under the banner of 'New Public Management', variable performance pay has been extended from the corporate to the public sector and beyond. In many or even most universities, professors are paid according to how much they publish, how often they get cited, and the amount of outside funds they attract.

At the same time, there is an elaborate system of honours and titles in academia to motivate scholars. The bestowal of honorary degrees has a long history, dating back at least to 1479, when the University of Oxford offered Lionel Woodville, Dean of Exeter and brother-in-law of Edward IV, an honorary degree. Notwithstanding their historic importance, there is still limited knowledge about the motivational consequences of awards on behaviour. Donors have just assumed their effect on performance to be positive.

However, this assumption has been disputed. Some would argue that awards are just a form of flattery, as they do not improve the material situation of their recipients. After all, awards cannot be consumed. They may simply be irrelevant to their recipients, or they may distract them from their actual work (e.g. leading academics to give talks at the expense of conducting further research). Even the presumed status effect of receiving an award can be called into question. Awards may put their winners in an uncomfortable situation where they have to face a large number of peers envying them, similar to the best pupil being ostracized from the class community. Awards can also attract the attention of critics who subsequently question the soundness of the jury's decision and publicly raise doubts about the recipients' merits. Moreover, the heightened attention can potentially give rise to choking under pressure, whereby the award recipients attempt to show that they merited the recognition, but the increased effort leads to worse performance and/or lower creativity. It is therefore an open question whether awards have any beneficial, performance-enhancing effect.

Motivations Behind the Bestowal of Academic Honours

Academic institutions bequeath awards for several different reasons. One is to publicly honour the most distinguished exponents in a particular academic field. The giving institutions, universities and scientific societies, can bask in the glory of famous award recipients. Quite another reason is to bind persons outside the academic system to a particular institution. For example, politicians are given honorary doctorates or honorary professorships, or wings and rooms are named after them, in order to thank them for their support. Similar awards are offered to thank donors for having contributed money, or to induce them to give money in the future. In the case of outsiders providing grants or endowments, the system can at times resemble a business deal in which academic awards are traded for monetary contributions. However, this is rarely, if ever, officially acknowledged because it would diminish the prestige of the giving institution and the awards it bestows. The academies receiving money from outside sources must make a great effort to remain in the scientific sphere devoted primarily to the pursuit of knowledge.

This chapter presents results from our analyses (Chan et al. 2014) on two highly esteemed awards given by academic institutions to honour economists for outstanding scientific performance. Such awards not only serve to acknowledge and highlight past achievements among peers but also to motivate award recipients to further pursue excellent research. At the same time, they can induce other members of academia to work hard in order to be awarded in the future. Our analyses focus on the implications of receiving an important academic award for their recipients' subsequent performance.

Two Prestigious Awards for Academic Economists

The first award we focus on is the John Bates Clark Medal, which is annually bequeathed by the American Economic Association to a scholar in the United States below the age of 40, 'who is judged to have made the most significant contribution to economic thought and knowledge'. A significant share of past Clark Medallists was later honoured with the Nobel Memorial Prize in Economic Sciences. Of the thirty-eight scholars who have been honoured with the Clark Medal as of 2016, twelve have subsequently won the Nobel Prize. Thanks to the age restriction, Clark Medallists are all of similar age and can be expected to have a long future academic life. This allows us to study the possible consequences of the award across an extended period of time.

The second prestigious academic award we analyse is election to Econometric Society Fellowship. Similar to Clark Medallists, scholars become Fellows relatively early in their careers (about fifteen years after their PhD). Yet, the selection mechanisms of the two awards are quite different. The choice of who becomes a Fellow is based on a vote among currently active members of the Econometric Society. In contrast, in the case of the Clark Medal, it is a small jury of prominent economists that decides on the winner.

For both academic awards, the set of comparable academics is unknown because shortlists are not made public. This further complicates any endeavour to distinguish the two links of causation. It is insufficient to establish that the recipients of the two awards publish more, and are cited more often, than other members of the academic community. The award winners may just be more able to begin with, which is why they have received the prize. This may explain why they also publish more and are cited more after having been awarded. In order to identify the possible effects on performance of receiving the John Bates Clark Medal, or of being appointed Econometric Society Fellow, the award recipients (the treatment group) must be compared to non-recipient scholars (the control group) with similar previous research performance and comparable career paths.

Identifying Causality with a Matching Approach

Using a fairly new econometric matching procedure, called the Synthetic Control Method, we seek to identify whether winning either of the two awards may raise research productivity and increase professional status. If so, we wish to know how large the performance differences are. We therefore look at publications as a proxy for productivity, and citations to papers published before the conferral as a proxy for the attention enjoyed in academic circles. By constructing a synthetic control group of economists and creating a twin for every award winner, we are able to compare the winners' performance to their performance had they not received the award. Based on the construction of such counterfactual scenarios of no award receipt, we aim to identify whether the bestowal of the Clark Medal or election as an Econometric Society Fellow simply reflect the past activity of particularly gifted economists, or whether the awards also seem to raise winners' subsequent productivity.

John Bates Clark Medallists

Data Employed

We use the publication and citation life-cycle profiles of researchers to create a dataset of elite economists and determine the most similar control group possible for the Clark Medallists. Publication content data of the top twenty-three economics and finance journals listed on the Web of Science are used as a basis. To capture all publications by both the Clark Medallists and the potential control group, we record the publication and yearly citation information on articles available in the selected journals up until December 2011. The resulting dataset consists of 26,523 unique researchers and 59,690 journal articles, of which 1,321 are authored by the first 34 Clark Medallists.

To construct a suitable comparison group for award winners we control for the quality of the education received because it may have an independent effect on being selected as a winner. It cannot be excluded that scholars educated at renowned universities have a better chance of getting the Medal. For that purpose, the rankings of economics departments are used to identify economists who received their doctoral degrees at institutions similar to, or the same as, those of the Clark Medallists. This information reduces the number of researchers to 10,093.

The number of quality-adjusted publications is taken as the measure of the productivity of a researcher. Citations per publication, controlling for the quality of the publication, are taken as the measure of professional recognition and status. To control for co-author influence, for each article the publication and citation counts are divided by the number of authors.

On average, a Clark Medallist had published a total of 17.7 articles the year before announcement of the award. The average age at which scholars in our dataset received the Clark Medal is 37.6 years. We focus on the first twenty-seven Clark Medallists (i.e. up to 2001) in order to have a sufficient timespan for assessing post-award performance. Table 4.1 provides the names and dates of birth of the winners of the John Bates Clark Medal for the twenty-seven bestowals considered.

Construction of the Synthetic Control Groups

The ideal method for assessing the effect of a prestigious academic award on its recipients' performance is to compare the winners' output after award receipt to the counterfactual scenario had they not won the award. To approximate such a comparison, we create two groups of synthetic counterfactuals using a weighted combination of researchers that best resemble the academic life-cycle of the corresponding medallist before receiving the award. Synthetic Control Group 1 is based on a pool of scholars that includes researchers who later received the John Bates Clark Medal; Synthetic Control Group 2 is based on a pool of scholars excluding those who later won the Clark Medal. Figure 4.1 shows that this was quite successfully achieved: the publications and citations of the winners and the control groups of non-winners are closely aligned before the date the Clark Medal was bequeathed to the winners.

Table 4.1 John Bates Clark Medallists, 1947–2001

John Bates Clark Medallists	Year Awarded	Year of Birth
Paul A. Samuelson	1947	1915
Kenneth E. Boulding	1949	1910
Milton Friedman	1951	1912
No award given	1953	
James Tobin	1955	1918
Kenneth J. Arrow	1957	1921
Lawrence R. Klein	1959	1920
Robert M. Solow	1961	1924
Hendrik S. Houthakker	1963	1924
Zvi Griliches	1965	1930
Gary S. Becker	1967	1930
Marc Nerlove	1969	1933
Dale W. Jorgenson	1971	1933
Franklin M. Fisher	1973	1934
Daniel L. McFadden	1975	1937
Martin S. Feldstein	1977	1939
Joseph E. Stiglitz	1979	1943
A. Michael Spence	1981	1943
James J. Heckman	1983	1944
Jerry A. Hausman	1985	1946
Sanford J. Grossman	1987	1953
David M. Kreps	1989	1950
Paul R. Krugman	1991	1953
Lawrence H. Summers	1993	1954
David Card	1995	1956
Kevin M. Murphy	1997	1958
Andrei Shleifer	1999	1961
Matthew Rabin	2001	1963

Notes: The list of all the John Bates Clark Medallists is provided by the American Economic Association, see http://www.aeaweb.org/honors_awards/clark_medal.php.

Publications

Figure 4.1 compares the average cumulative publication trajectory for Clark Medallists with that of the Synthetic Control Groups. Five years after the award, medallists have on average achieved 9.26 weighted publications, which is 1.05 more than the 8.21 weighted publications of the Synthetic Control Group 1. This is an increase of about 13 per cent. The difference between the treatment and Control Group 1 grows to 1.42 weighted publications ten years after award conferral, when medallists and the synthetic control group have on average published 10.75 and 9.32 weighted articles, respectively. This is an increase of more than 15 per cent. The results are quite similar for the Synthetic Control Group 2.

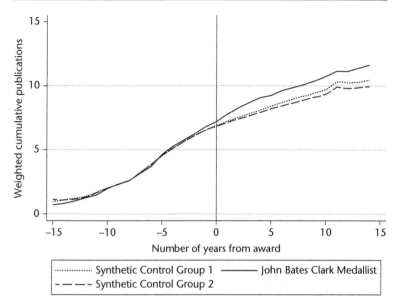

Figure 4.1 Number of publications, Clark Medallists

Whether the increase in post-award publications is due to increased effort, more resources for research, or to a higher facility for medallists to move past referees and editors is open for debate. All three reasons may be relevant. The recipients of the Clark Medal may enjoy higher self-confidence inducing them to work even harder, it is likely that they get additional resources from their universities and outside sources, they possibly attract more and better co-workers, and because they are better known than before they may have improved publication chances. The latter possibility would correspond to the Matthew effect, whereby the 'rich get richer' merely because of the higher status they have reached.

Citations

The pre-award publications by Clark Medallists also draw significantly more citations than those by the synthetic counterfactuals. Figure 4.2 again shows that the citation paths for both synthetic groups are practically identical and do not significantly differ in the pre-award period, indicating a close match in the pre-award quality measure. The citations to pre-award journal publications then diverge once Clark Medallists experience the status change in the year the Clark Medal is conferred.

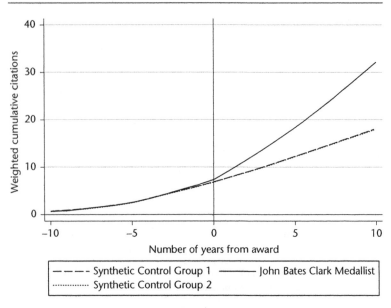

Figure 4.2 Citations per publication, Clark Medallists

On average, medallists have received 18.36 citations for each pre-award publication five years after award conferral, and 32.12 after ten years. Synthetic Control Group 1 has only received 12.27 and 18.1 citations by then, respectively. In other words, compared to the Synthetic Control Group 1, five and ten years after the award bestowal, medallists have received 6.09 and 14.02 more citations, respectively, for any article they had published before receiving the award. The respective increases amount to 50 and 78 per cent.

Looking at the post-award citation rates over a longer time horizon than ten years shows that the differentials persist and become even more pronounced (in this case Synthetic Control Groups 1 and 2 are identical). In every year, from year 11 to year 20 after award bestowal, the gap between the groups grows in later post-award years, reaching the largest relative difference twenty years after the award (3.07 times more citations for medallists).

These results may be considered surprising if one believes that an article is cited solely because of its intrinsic value to scholarship. Such a view is, however, unrealistic, as these and other results suggest. The papers written by economists before getting the Clark Medal are cited more, presumably because the respective scholar is better known and because the content of an article is more highly appreciated as the writer gets this prestigious award thereafter. This observation is consistent with a status (or Matthew) effect.

The attention-conferring effect of awards could be crucial in explaining the strong contrast we find between treatment and control groups. Academia is faced with a 'battle for attention' due to the great number of papers produced each year. Since the sheer number of researchers and articles makes it difficult to assess quality, awards can assume an important signalling function. The copious output may lead scholars to rely on simple heuristics for information gathering and might explain why economists are attracted by the fame of prestigious awards.

Fellowship of the Econometric Society

In order to analyse whether prestigious awards are positively related to future performance, we additionally consider a quite different type of honour in academia, being appointed Fellow of the Econometric Society. This Fellowship is taken to be a great distinction and is highly regarded among economists. Over nine hundred individuals have so far been awarded an Econometric Society Fellowship.

The Fellows should be chosen on the basis of their merit. The effect of the Fellowship on performance cannot be identified with conventional methods, as performance differentials may be due to the higher ability of the Fellows appointed. Since the shortlists of possible Fellows are not publicly available it is not possible to compare the performance of Fellows with that of similar persons not winning the distinction. The Synthetic Control Method again allows us to construct a control group of unelected scholars whose publication and citation records closely mirror the Fellows' records prior to election.

Our analysis considers Fellows elected between five and twenty-five years after the year that their first publication appeared in the dataset, and where the election was made between 1945 and 1990. The first of the limitations ensures sufficient pre-treatment observations for the matching process. The second criterion enables us to examine the status effect through comparison of post-treatment publication activity for at least fifteen years. Of the 463 Fellows elected during the 1945–90 period, 88 are excluded because of the first restriction, leaving a sample size of 375.

Publications

The publication output and citations of Econometric Society Fellows is again outlined in graphs. These depict the success of the group of

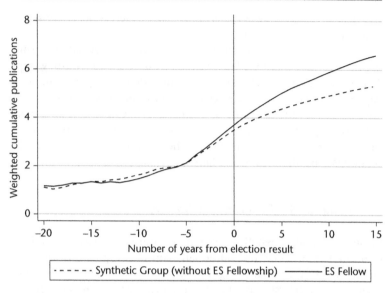

Figure 4.3 Publication counts, Econometric Society Fellows

Econometric Society Fellows compared to the synthetic non-Fellow group, and allow us to compare their scholarly performance in the post-award period.

Figure 4.3 plots the cumulative publication counts for Econometric Society Fellows and the Synthetic Control Group. In the pre-award period, both Fellows and the Synthetic Control Group share a similar publication performance. After the election, however, the two paths diverge markedly, indicating an increase in productivity levels that is attributable to the Fellowship. For Fellows, the total weighted publications are 5.02 and 5.89 at five and ten years after election, respectively, whereas for the Synthetic Control Group they are 4.38 and 4.93, respectively. The publication activity has thus increased by 15 per cent five years after receiving the award, and by 19 per cent ten years thereafter. This post-award publication performance difference grows over time.

Several reasons can be adduced to explain the increasing publication difference. It seems reasonable to assume that an average researcher is not aware of who is an Econometric Society Fellow and who is not. Thus, a well-founded explanation has to consider factors pertaining to an individual Fellow. First, the honour received may have a positive motivational effect, for instance due to increased enthusiasm. Second, being elected a Fellow may bolster self-confidence, which enhances motivation and can thus increase productivity. Third, the newly elected Fellows may take other Econometric Society Fellows as a reference group and accordingly make an effort to keep up with them. Although 'outsiders' might on average not be aware of who is an Econometric Society Fellow, Fellows themselves are likely to compare themselves to their peers. Given that many Econometric Society Fellows sit on editorial boards of journals, this might also affect the chances of a Fellow to be accepted or invited for publication in the respective journal. Moreover, the formation of productive research collaborations might be enhanced, as the Fellowship status serves as a signal of high quality towards other researchers—be they Fellows themselves or not. By the same signalling mechanism, the award may also make available more financial resources, such as research grants.

Citations

Figure 4.4 illustrates the weighted cumulative citations per publication for articles published before award conferral, comparing the work of Fellows with that of the Synthetic Control Group. Assuming that article quality was revealed in the pre-award timeframe, it follows that both the treatment and control groups' publications have the same or similar

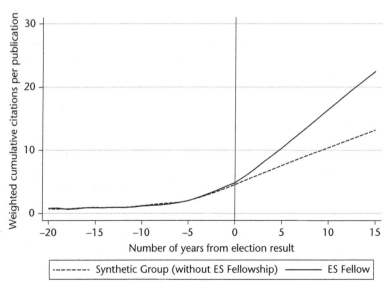

Figure 4.4 Citations per publication, Econometric Society Fellows

ex ante quality. Any ex post difference in citation performance thus reflects the status effect of becoming a Fellow. Like the productivity measures, the citations per publication paths evolve similarly for both the treatment and control groups until the announcement of the election result, after which citation differences indicate an immediate status effect. That means becoming a Fellow is accompanied by an increase in citations to articles published before the election.

Five and ten years after the election, Fellows have on average received a total of 10.4 and 16.52 quality-adjusted citations for each article published before announcement of the election result. The synthetic counterfactuals, in contrast, have only received 7.58 and 10.45 citations per publication by then, respectively. This means that, five years after the election, Econometric Society Fellows have received 37 per cent more citations per pre-award publication than had they not become Fellows. After another five years, this difference has risen to 58 per cent (all estimates being statistically significant at the 1 per cent level). This suggests that an increase in fame enhances citation success. At least some researchers become aware of the newly elected Fellow's work and hence start to cite it.

The Matching Method

Our methodological approach provides a way of analysing the consequences of receiving awards. The use of the Synthetic Control Method has limitations, though. A methodological concern is that the award-giving committee might have information at its disposal that we cannot identify and integrate into the matching procedure. While we control for candidates' work in the pipeline, the committee might be able to assess their potential future performance based on other, non-observable determinants.

However, this claim only applies to expected future publications. It does not hold for citations to work published before receiving the award. It would be a fluke if the past publications of scholars were suddenly cited more often, coincidentally after receiving the Clark Medal or being elected Econometric Society Fellow. It is more plausible to attribute this belated citation surge to getting one of these much-esteemed awards.

The case of Econometric Society Fellowship provides another argument why the jury's possible superior insights regarding candidates' future performance seem insufficient to fully explain the performance differentials we observe. It is quite unlikely that the 470 Fellows who are presently allowed to vote on new Fellows are able to come to a shared opinion about a scholar's future performance, above and beyond the candidate's past publications and citations. This general election process goes far beyond the private deliberations in a small jury setting, which may have informed the choice of Clark Medallists.

The Fields Medal in Mathematics

A recent study by Borjas and Doran (2015) of the Fields Medal, the top mathematics prize for scholars under the age of 40, points to a distorting effect awards can have on their winners' performance. The study indicates that the Fields Medallists' publication rate subsequently declines compared to that of non-winning contenders. This result at first glance seems to contradict our findings. It may, however, be explained by the fact that the Fields Medal is the very peak in a mathematician's career— especially as there is no Nobel Prize in mathematics. Fields Medallists' excellence has been so well established that they are not forced to pursue the normal course of research as reflected in measures conventionally used to judge performance, namely, publications. Rather, they are free to turn their attention to new and possibly more risky topics attracting their current interest. In contrast, Clark Medallists and Econometric Society Fellows have a good chance of receiving the Nobel Prize in the future. Receiving the Clark Medal or being elected Fellow may encourage scholars to concentrate on doing research instead of engaging in, say, administrative or outside consulting work. Their institutions are likely to encourage them in this direction. Our results support this conjecture.

Conclusions

Identifying the causal effect of honours on their winners' future performance is difficult since awards are given for outstanding achievements. Observing that award winners subsequently outperform others does not allow us to draw causal inferences as to the award's total effects on performance. It cannot, in principle, be excluded that the mere fact that awards were handed out may have even had a negative effect on subsequent scholarly performance. This seems to be quite unlikely, as we observe that the publications and citations of both winners and non-winners of the Clark Medal and Econometric Society Fellowship increased over time (see Figures 4.1 to 4.4). Nevertheless, it cannot be excluded that the performance could have increased even more in the absence of any awards.

We have adduced two major reasons for why awards may raise performance: they increase their recipients' motivation, or they provoke a status (or Matthew) effect.

Academic institutions have multiple reasons for bestowing awards. These include basking in reflected glory, establishing ties to the recipient (e.g. to politicians or donors), and, of course, motivating scholars to perform better. Notwithstanding the frequent use of awards in academia, the effects on their winners' performance have rarely been empirically analysed.

This chapter analysed the performance effects of two prestigious awards given to academic economists, the John Bates Clark Medal and the Fellowship of the Econometric Society. Table 4.2 summarizes the results.

We find that Clark Medallists publish considerably more articles, and that their previous work draws many more citations than in the counterfactual scenario of no award receipt. To be appointed as an Econometric Society Fellow also seems to strongly raise the publication rate, and Fellows' past work draws many more citations than had they not been elected Fellows.

Generalizing these results, our analyses suggest a performance- and status-enhancing effect of awards. Receiving a prestigious honour may induce winners to work harder. It can also raise the likelihood of getting grants, teaching releases, better students, and new and productive co-authors, thereby also increasing productivity. The increased attention received from other scholars positively affects the winners' status. Based on our empirical findings covering two different awards bequeathed by two different academic societies, we suggest that prestigious academic honours tend to raise productivity in terms of publications, and attract more attention as reflected in an increased number of citations to winners' previous work.

Table 4.2 Comparison of award winners' performance with Synthetic Control Group after five and ten years

		Clark Medallists	Ecm. Soc. Fellows
Publication	5 years	13%	15%
	10 years	15%	19%
Citations	5 years	50%	37%
	10 years	78%	58%

Related Literature

This chapter is based on, and closely follows, a joint paper with Benno Torgler and Ho Fai Chan, titled 'Academic Honors and Performance' (Chan et al. 2014). The data-driven approach to construct Synthetic Control Groups was developed by Abadie and Gardeazabal (2003). For our identification of status effects we rely on Azoulay et al. (2013), using the flow of citations to previously published work as a metric for status effects. A groundbreaking contribution to the literature on status effects in science, which introduced the synonymous term 'Matthew effect', was Merton (1968).

In our paper, we also include a number of robustness tests. Moreover, we approach the question of whether the increase in post-award publications is more likely to be due to increased effort, or to a higher facility for award recipients to move past referees and editors.

Publications and citation counts as a measure of scholars' influence in societal discourse are discussed and empirically analysed in Chan et al. (2015). The bestowal of honorary degrees has a long tradition in academia. The Oxford University Archives (2013) present an interesting article on the subject.

Scepticism about the value of awards to their recipients is referenced in Besley (2005). Marie Curie, who is among the four persons having received two Nobel Prizes and the only one having won the Prize in two different sciences, famously stated: 'En sciences, nous devons nous intéresser aux choses, non aux personnes.' ('In science, we should be interested in facts, not in people.') This quote can be found in various literary sources, such as the biography written by her daughter, Eve Curie (1938, p. 171).

The Economist (2004) even ridicules awards and decorations, proclaiming that such distinctions in fact kill the recipient's honour rather than increasing it. In an empirical study of literary awards, Kovács and Sharkey (2014) show that award winners' increased popularity can paradoxically cause more negative rather than positive evaluations of their quality.

Econometric Society Fellowship also is the focus of some other studies. Chan and Torgler (2012) point out that of the sixty-nine scholars who had received the economics Nobel Prize before 2011, only nine had not also been made Fellows of the Econometric Society. Hamermesh and Schmidt (2003) investigate whether the elections to Econometric Society Fellowship are fair, i.e. whether they are based solely on the candidates' quality. The analysis shows that the choices, at least in the past, were also influenced by characteristics unrelated to quality, such as a researcher's geographic location or subspeciality.

5

Awards in the Voluntary Sector

Reasons for Using Awards

Awards play a prominent role in the voluntary sector. There are five major reasons why the bestowal of honours is of strategic importance for non-profit organizations. First, non-profit organizations are often strongly cash constrained. They have to find other means than money to motivate people to contribute their time and effort. Second, intrinsic motivation constitutes a major reason to engage as a volunteer. Any extrinsic rewards must therefore be employed with caution, to not crowd out this form of motivation. We argue that awards are less likely than money to provoke a crowding-out effect, and that they may even support intrinsic motivation. Third, social recognition is another important motive for volunteering. The bestowal of an award is a form of social recognition, which is communicated in front of an audience and therefore sends a stronger signal than private words of praise (or transfers of money). Fourth, award ceremonies provide a festive occasion at which members of the organization (volunteers alongside paid workers) as well as outside partners (e.g. from other voluntary organizations, politicians, and sponsors) can celebrate and establish social ties. While an award is often given to a specific person, donors frequently make clear that the gratitude extends to all the volunteers, and that the contributions of all of them are being recognized. As a result, a larger group of volunteers may feel appreciated for their efforts. Finally, the publicity of awards and award ceremonies can be used to increase the visibility of volunteering in society and attract new volunteers.

Types of Awards in the Third Sector

A great variety of different awards can be observed in the non-profit and humanitarian sectors. Besides the Nobel Peace Prize, which is probably the most renowned specimen, there is an uncountable number of other honours lauding citizens for their engagement. A nice example is the Order of the Smile, an international award given by children and recognized by the United Nations. The order honours adults for their exemplary engagement for children. It includes among its recipients such eminent personalities as Pope John Paul II, Mother Teresa, the 14th Dalai Lama, Astrid Lindgren, and Steven Spielberg.

Famous third-sector organizations such as Caritas or Amnesty International hand out awards to make their cause visible and to motivate their members. The International Committee of the Red Cross bestows the Florence Nightingale Medal to nurses and nursing aides to recognize their 'exceptional courage and devotion to victims of armed conflict or natural disaster'. National Red Cross organizations also employ awards, such as the Blood Donation Medal (*Medaille für Verdienste um das Blutspenden*) or the Service Medal (*Verdienstmedaille*) given by the Austrian Red Cross. In the United Kingdom, the British Red Cross Humanitarian Citizen Awards are given to young volunteers under the age of 25.

Heads of state around the world bestow awards to signal their support and encourage citizens to engage in pro-social behaviour. In the United Kingdom, The Queen's Award for Voluntary Service is an esteemed national honour given to groups of volunteers for their contributions to local communities. Its status is officially recognized to be equivalent to that of the MBE (Member of the Most Excellent Order of the British Empire) for individuals. Winners receive a certificate signed by the Queen and a commemorative crystal, both presented by Her Majesty's local Lord-Lieutenants. Moreover, they have the opportunity to attend one of Her Majesty's garden parties at Buckingham Palace.

In the United States, the President's Volunteer Service Award is meant 'to thank and honor Americans who, by their demonstrated commitment and example, inspire others to engage in volunteer service'. The value of this award to the recipient certainly outweighs the monetary costs to the giver. As one learns on the official website, the award package, including award pin, personalized certificate of achievement, and congratulatory letter from the President, costs between 2 US dollars (about 1 British pound, or 1.50 euros) and 4.75 US dollars (2.80 British pounds, or 3.55 euros).

Table 5.1 Awards in the voluntary and humanitarian sectors (selection)

Award	Presented by	First bestowal	Number of recipients
Supranational level			
Nobel Peace Prize	Norwegian Nobel Committee	1901	Limited
Florence Nightingale Medal	International Committee of the Red Cross	1920	Open, but bestowal highly selective
Order of the Smile	Children	1968	Limited
Sakharov Prize	European Parliament	1988	Limited
National level			
The Queen's Badge of Honour	British Red Cross	1958	Limited
Medaille für Verdienste um das Blutspenden des Österreichischen Roten Kreuzes	Austrian Red Cross	1969	Open, but tied to exact criteria
The Queen's Award for Voluntary Service	The local Lord-Lieutenant or Lieutenant-Governor, on behalf of the Queen	2003	Limited
President's Volunteer Service Award (US)	Approved Certifying Organizations	2003	Open
German Prize for Civic Engagement	Alliance of third-sector organizations, supported also by a Federal Ministry	2009	Limited
Subnational level			
Bavarian Order of Merit	Prime Minister of the State of Bavaria	1957	Limited

Table 5.1 provides an overview of selected awards handed out in the non-profit sector. As can be seen, they cover a wide range of activities and organizations and they differ substantially from each other. These awards are given at a supranational, national, and subnational level.

The great use made of awards in the voluntary sector is not only due to cash constraints. Even if non-profit organizations and public-sector officials had sufficient funds at hand to show their appreciation via material or even monetary gifts, such action would risk being considered inappropriate. Using money to induce contributions to a good cause can undermine exactly the motivation on which voluntary contributions are based.

Voluntary Contributions to Wikipedia

With more than 43 million encyclopaedic articles in more than 280 different languages (as of December 2016), Wikipedia is the largest online encyclopaedia and one of the most often frequented websites worldwide. It is almost entirely based on voluntary contributions, and yet only four years after its creation Wikipedia's quality was considered to be on a par with that of the Encyclopaedia Britannica.

As of December 2016, more than 65 million registered editors had voluntarily contributed to Wikipedia. These astonishing participation rates confront economists with a puzzle. According to standard economic theory, not a single person should have contributed to this project. A self-interested homo oeconomicus would have little reason to contribute to Wikipedia since this activity is not remunerated. Wikipedia editors (or 'users', as they are called on Wikipedia) do not even gain a reputational advantage in the non-virtual world since they contribute under pseudonyms. In most cases, editors' relevant peer groups are unaware of their virtuous engagement online. Roundtables of Wikipedia editors (or 'Wikipedians' for the more committed ones) do exist, but only a minor fraction of editors actually attends them. When they do, interesting situations can arise, where people know each other's faces but not their real names. Some editors indicate their names, while others explicitly do not reveal their non-virtual identities and just refer others to their online pseudonym ('user name').

Declining Retention Rates

The recognition accruing to editors is also considerably reduced by the nature of Wikipedia work, where multiple authors work on an article, so that it is difficult to see who was responsible for a particularly well-written part. While editors' contributions are easily and at times quickly reverted (made undone) or changed, instances of praise remain rather limited in comparison. The demotivating effect this can have has been recognized and technical changes (e.g. the introduction of a 'thanks' button) have been made to facilitate editors to give each other positive feedback as well. Yet, for new editors unfamiliar with the many rules and guidelines the community has evolved over the years, reverts and warning messages remain frequent. Moreover, discussions on the so-called 'talk pages' can have a discouragingly harsh tone. This may explain in part why Wikipedia has been increasingly struggling with declining editor retention rates, particularly among newcomers.

The trend of declining retention rates is emblematic of a wider trend observable in the third sector. Volunteers are increasingly unwilling or unable to commit to an organization for a longer period of time. Hence, voluntary organizations and state officials wanting to promote sustained voluntary engagement are confronted with the question of how to motivate people to continue their engagement. Unlike firms, they cannot readily rely on contracts or conventional incentive schemes (e.g. variable performance pay). They have to find more subtle ways than promising a carrot (incentive) to make the volunteer go 'the extra mile'. Instead, they can focus on what volunteers have done particularly well and highlight past achievements, hoping that this will encourage more of the same behaviour in the future. One way of doing this is by giving praise and positive feedback. Another way consists in making the appraisal public by giving an award for exemplary commitment. This sends a stronger signal than private words of praise.

Based on a field experiment at Wikipedia (Gallus 2016), we investigate the latter option in this chapter. We want to see whether purely symbolic awards can motivate new editors to stay active.

A Large-Scale Field Experiment on Purely Symbolic Awards

The analysis of whether awards are able to motivate volunteers to sustain their contributions is confronted with the same major obstacle that we have observed in the case of honours in academia discussed in Chapter 4. Since awards are given for outstanding behaviour, causality cannot be established. As it is 'the best' or most motivated who are awarded, it is not surprising that award recipients also perform better, or are more motivated, than other persons in the future. Observing award recipients' superior performance does not allow us to conclude that it was the award as such that raised the performance.

When analysing the effects of awards on performance in academia in Chapter 4, we constructed a comparison group using the Synthetic Control Method. Another strategy for identifying causal effects is to use randomization. Since established award juries are reluctant to adopt this approach, a new award scheme had to be implemented, with a committee of senior practitioners to establish the award's reputation (see Table A1 in the online appendix to Gallus 2016, available as supplemental material at http://dx.doi.org/10.1287/mnsc.2016.2540).

Besides cleanly identifying causality in a natural context, the field experiment also made it possible to deal with another major obstacle commonly encountered when studying awards: that awards are often accompanied by material or monetary prizes, and that they tend to provide career-related benefits that may result in higher earnings in the future. This makes it difficult to argue that any motivational effect one may find can be traced back to the symbolic nature of the awards (i.e. the public recognition), rather than the pecuniary benefits they entail. The context of Wikipedia makes it possible to examine the causal effects of awards while ruling out material and career-related benefits that awards might otherwise entail; individuals tend to operate anonymously under pseudonyms.

Experimental Design

The field experiment proceeded in four steps. First, on the 6th of every month, a data dump of the German language Wikipedia was obtained, which identified editors and their contributions. A computer script was used to identify all new editors who had made their first edit to an article in the previous month (approximately three thousand) and submit them to a basic screening, whereby algorithms singled out those editors who were not blocked and who had contributed at least twice, with a minimum of five days between their first and last edits. This increased the chances that editors would actually return to their account and see that they had received an award (if they belonged to the treatment group).

Second, the remaining editors (approximately five hundred) were examined one by one to exclude vandals, advertisers, secondary accounts ('sockpuppets'), group accounts (including those created by organizations), and accounts of Wikimedia employees according to a rulebook developed for this purpose. For this step, an algorithm had been developed that flagged an editor if specific keywords were found on his or her personal Wikipedia page ('user page'). Only editors were retained who had made at least one contribution to an article that was still visible at the day of the screening, i.e. that had not been deleted. The careful screening process had been developed in consultation with experienced community members. It helped ensure that members of the resulting pool of candidates would in principle all have deserved a small newcomer award for their first efforts to contribute to Wikipedia.

From the pool of remaining editors (approximately 370), 150 award recipients were randomly selected (treatment group). In a fourth and last step, on the morning of the 12th of the given month, the list of winners was posted on the award's page and a text accompanied by a graphic award was placed on the awardees' discussion ('talk') pages, informing them that there had been over four thousand newcomers, i.e. potential candidates, in the previous month (see Figure A.2 in the appendix to Gallus 2016). A Wikipedia account bearing the name of the award had been created for the purpose of making these posts, which were publicly visible.

The award scheme studied in this experiment closely mirrors institutionalized award schemes as observed in other fields, with regular intervals, fixed numbers, repeated bestowals over a long-term horizon, a hall of fame, a reputable jury, and the prestige of a national portal; these attributes clearly differentiate the awards from personal feedback or other informal rewards.

Results

The experimental design permits a straightforward identification of causality using basic mean-comparison tests (randomization checks are provided in Table 1 in Gallus 2016). The analysis considers eleven awarding rounds, from September 2012 to July 2013. Each month, 150 newcomers received the 'Edelweiss with Star' award. As of May 2015, when the latest data dump was received, thirty-three editors (2 per cent) from the treatment group and seventy-seven editors (3 per cent) from the control group had been blocked since the awarding date and thus dropped out of the dataset. Treatment and control groups therefore comprise 1,617 and 2,390 editors, respectively (Table A1 in the online appendix to Gallus 2016 gives an overview of the monthly cohorts).

General Activity

First, the main results from this field experiment demonstrate that purely symbolic awards without any material value motivate new editors to continue their voluntary engagement. Figure 5.1 plots the shares of editors in the control and treatment groups who become active again in the four weeks following the awarding date. This basic bar chart indicates that the retention rate is seven percentage points higher for recipients of the award. The error bars indicate that the 20 per cent increase in the retention rate is statistically significant.

Table 5.2 reports the retention rates in the treatment and control groups, as well as the differences between them and the p-values resulting from the Chi-square tests. Panel A focuses on the most basic measure of retention, i.e. whether any activity can be observed after the awarding date. Following Figure 5.1, the first row considers the four weeks after the awarding date and shows that the difference observed in the

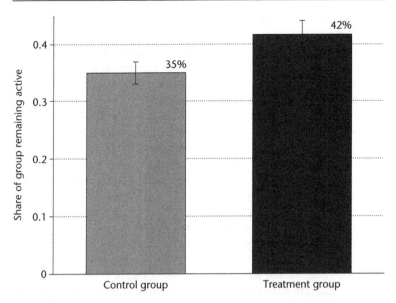

Figure 5.1 Mean retention rates of award recipients compared to a control group with no award

Notes: Shows the month after awarding date. The black error bars indicate the respective 95 per cent confidence intervals. See Gallus (2016), Figure 1.

Interpretation: This basic bar chart indicates that the retention rate is about 7 percentage points higher for award recipients. The error bars indicate that this 20 per cent increase in the retention rate is statistically significant.

Table 5.2 Retention effect

	Treatment (1)	Control (2)	Difference (3)
A. General activity			
Active (1st month)	0.42	0.35	0.07*** (0.000)
Active (following 2 months)	0.49	0.43	0.06*** (0.000)
B. Direct content provision			
Active, only article edits (1st month)	0.36	0.32	0.04* (0.017)
Active, only article edits (2 months)	0.43	0.40	0.04* (0.022)
N	1,617	2,390	4,007

Notes: This table reports the retention rates in the treatment and control groups, the differences between them, and the *p*-values resulting from Chi-square tests (in parentheses). Average values are rounded to 2 decimal places. Adjustments for multiple comparisons using the procedure and code developed by List et al. (2016) do not change the significance of any of the tests (see Table B2 in the online appendix to Gallus 2016). *$p < 0.05$; ***$p < 0.001$.

Source: Gallus 2016.

bar chart is indeed statistically significant at the 99.9 per cent level ($p = 0.000$).

Row 2 in panel A (Table 5.2) extends the period of observation to the two months following the intervention to ascertain that the difference that can be observed in row 1 is not due to a temporal substitution effect (i.e. that award recipients do not merely advance their next period of activity to the first month instead of the second month after the awarding date). The results in row 2 confirm that, when considering the two months following the intervention, the retention rate in the treatment group continues to exceed the retention rate in the control group by six percentage points (49 versus 43 per cent). This treatment effect of 14 per cent is again highly statistically significant ($p = 0.000$). The award's effect on retention is thus not due to editors resuming their activity earlier than usual because of the award.

Even when considering only direct contributions to articles (and not, for example, participation in discussions), the effect persists (see Table 5.1 Panel B). The award increases the share of winners remaining active in this dimension of work by 13 per cent (from 32 to 36 per cent; $p = 0.017$).

The analysis in Gallus (2016) furthermore looks at the effect of the award on the degree of article editing activity to assure that the effect found on retention is not driven by only minor article editing activity. Figure 2 in Gallus (2016) depicts the award's treatment effect at each level of article editing activity. It shows that the award not only lowers the attrition rate of new authors, but that it raises the share of editors at every level of activity.

Treatment Effect Persistence

The focus of the analysis lies on the four weeks after the awarding date. However, we can draw on a supplementary analysis that further extends the period of observation to get an indication of whether the difference in retention rates between the treatment and control groups also persists over the long term. Table 5.3 shows that, when considering the retention rates in the quarters following the initial award, the difference between treatment and control groups persists and remains significant until and including the fourth quarter after the intervention. Whether on its own or together with reinforcing feedback dynamics, the award provokes an increase in the retention rate by 11 per cent (from 47 to 52 per cent; $p = 0.002$), 10 per cent (from 31 to 34 per cent; $p = 0.032$), 13 per cent (from 24 to 27 per cent; $p = 0.031$), and 13 per cent (from 23 to 26 per cent; $p = 0.037$) in quarters 1, 2, 3, and 4, respectively, after the

Table 5.3 Persistence of treatment effect

	Treatment (1)	Control (2)	Difference (3)
General activity			
Quarter 1	0.52	0.47	0.05** (0.002)
Quarter 2	0.34	0.31	0.03* (0.032)
Quarter 3	0.27	0.24	0.03* (0.031)
Quarter 4	0.26	0.23	0.03* (0.037)
Quarter 5	0.21	0.20	0.02 (0.221)
N	1,617	2,390	4,007

Notes: This table reports the retention rates in the treatment and control groups, the differences between them, and the p-values resulting from Chi-square tests (in parentheses). Average values are rounded to 2 decimal places. The table shows that the difference in the retention rates continues to be statistically significant in the four quarters following the initial intervention. There were two higher-level awards (Edelweiss with two and three stars), which winners of the first award (Edelweiss with star) could get; they could be received after months 2 and 5 after the initial award whose effects are being tested. The scheme included no further awards thereafter. *$p < 0.05$; **$p < 0.01$.

Source: Gallus 2016.

intervention. The difference in quarter 5 still points in the expected direction but it is no longer significant ($p = 0.221$).

There is so far only limited evidence on the post-intervention persistence of treatment effects in the context of voluntary public goods contributions. The related field experiments that do consider long-run post-intervention implications (six months and longer) mostly study treatments targeted at charitable giving, and environmental conservation interventions using household-level social comparison messages (see Gallus 2016, p. 10). The results of these studies are mixed; while in some cases the effects persist after the treatment's discontinuation, in other cases they vanish or even turn into negative net effects, for instance due to motivation crowding-out. Given their significant costs, some interventions end up destroying more value than they might have initially created. Symbolic awards are a low-cost intervention. The basic test in Table 5.3 helps ensure that the positive effect found in the first month after the award bestowal is not reversed later on. The finding that the retention rate in the treatment group continues to lie significantly above that in the control group in each of the following four quarters indicates that awards have the potential to trigger a dynamic that fosters retention over the long term.

Accounting for the Treatment Effects

There are various mechanisms through which even purely symbolic awards can have a positive effect on newcomer retention. The relevance of four major explanations is tested. First, the awards seem to encourage newcomers to self-identify with the community, making them feel that they are part of this online group of 'Wikipedians' (see Gallus 2016, p. 11 for the data and analysis). Second, at least for some award recipients, the awards cater to status and reputation concerns, which may account for part of their motivating effect. The awards lend the newcomers reputational capital within the online community they have recently joined. Third, a substantial number of newcomers refer in particular to the recognition provided through these awards as a major source of motivation. For some, the recognition for their first efforts seems to have bolstered their self-confidence in this critical learning stage. Feeling more confident that one's contributions add value may be motivating in itself. Lastly, related to the recognition-based explanation, awards also signal to their recipients that their individual inputs for the common good are being identified and evaluated by others. Recipients no longer feel 'lost in the crowd' and instead experience that they receive credit for their inputs.

The relevance of this explanation is supported by responses illustrating that some individuals clearly attribute their award receipt to specific contributions they have made, which they perceive to have been evaluated. For instance, one recipient wrote to his mentor:

> I received an award from the Portal Switzerland *for my first article* (Edelweiss with a Star)!! I want to thank you most warmly for mentoring me, since I would not have succeeded in writing the article like that without your help during my first Wiki-steps. As such, a petal of the edelweiss belongs to you; just choose one. Again, thank you and I look forward to our future cooperation! (September 2012; emphasis added)

Awards Support Voluntary Engagement

The analysis of the field experiment at Wikipedia reveals that awards can have a considerable, statistically highly significant, and sustainable positive effect on retention. This holds even though the awards are given in a pseudonymous context where no material or non-virtual benefits such as status among established peers could arise. The award recipients are newcomers who have barely started to interact with the community of Wikipedians.

The findings are noteworthy also because the Wikipedia awards are costless. Even organizations running on low budgets thus have powerful motivators at their disposal, as this chapter shows. Awards need not carry monetary prize purses to be taken seriously and to have an effect. This is the first field experiment we are aware of that tests the effectiveness of institutionalized award schemes, with regular monthly intervals, a fixed number of recipients, a proper award jury of senior community members, and a hall of fame-like award page giving the awards an official nature.

The estimates of the awards' effects are conservative since non-responsiveness to the awards may have been due to indifference, but also to unawareness; some recipients simply do not return to their own page and thus do not see that they have won an award. Moreover, possible spillover effects of the awards on third parties are left aside. Some recipients, for instance, wrote to other editors (often their mentors), thanking them for their support. Hence, the awards' beneficial effects may have well exceeded the effects found in the analysis.

Nonetheless, one has to be aware of the limitations of using awards. Organizations can only distribute awards in limited quantities since their value hinges on them being held in scarce supply. Integrating awards into a broader recognition scheme also involving other rewards such as presents or invitations to events is advisable. Organizations should moreover endeavour to leverage their awards' effects by highlighting that the recipients are to be seen as representatives of all the other volunteers engaging in similarly praiseworthy activities. This is an important aspect and potentially spreads the reach of the motivating effects of awards.

Conclusions

Although research on the motivations for private contributions to public goods is extensive, little is known about the rewards that help sustain volunteers' contributions without crowding out their intrinsic and image motivations. Awards such as orders and medals of valour are symbolic rewards that may foster such voluntary behaviour. They are a widespread phenomenon, as the introduction to this chapter shows. However, any investigation into their causal effects is hindered by their juries' reluctance to see their authority replaced by random decision-making processes.

This chapter presents a large-scale natural field experiment in which an award scheme with fixed intervals and award numbers is institutionalized and randomization is employed to establish clear causal effects of awards on voluntary contributions to the public good Wikipedia. The experiment addresses one of the online encyclopaedia's most serious challenges, the retention of new editors. Retention (or turnover) is an interesting issue to study also because so many organizations struggle with it.

The field experiment shows that purely symbolic awards can be used to increase newcomer retention, even if the status and reputational capital they provide are limited to an online community the award recipient has only recently joined. The award scheme is shown to have a considerable and statistically highly significant effect on retention. It increases the share of newcomers who remain active in the four weeks after the awarding date by 20 per cent, from a share of 35 per cent to one of 42 per cent. A supplementary analysis of treatment effect persistence indicates that the difference in retention rates between control and treatment groups continues to be significant over the four quarters after the intervention. It becomes insignificant thereafter (although the difference still points in the expected direction). The discussion considers four major explanations for the motivational effect of the symbolic awards: increased self-identification as a community member, status and reputational concerns, recognition, and others' attention (not feeling lost in the crowd). Additional data (e.g. on social signalling) as well as anecdotal evidence support the relevance of these explanations.

The findings are worth noting not only because the award is costless and has no material implications, but also because it is given to newcomers who operate under pseudonyms that they have only recently adopted. Honours seem to provide volunteer organizations with a mechanism to 'pull in' newcomers. The same may be true for established members as well, in that a long-tenured volunteer is probably reluctant to quit her engagement shortly after receiving a public recognition. This, however, still needs to be tested in future research. There may likely be groups of individuals (e.g. based on tenure, the degree of involvement, age, and gender) who are particularly responsive to receiving awards.

Since awards have to be used sparingly to prevent inflationary tendencies, it would be useful to know whom to target more specifically. This, of course, also implies that we need a better understanding of how non-recipients (who may receive an award in the future) respond, and how awards should be designed to produce positive external effects on these third parties (e.g. thanks to basking in the recipients' reflected glory).

Future research could usefully inform the design and use of award schemes for volunteers by examining such third-party effects and possible heterogeneity in the responsiveness to awards. It should also analyse more closely the boundary conditions of this study, and how awards interact with other rewards and incentives (e.g. personal praise, thank you gifts, and communal events).

Related Literature

This chapter is based on Gallus (2016). Another Wikipedia field experiment (Restivo and van de Rijt 2012) explores informal peer-to-peer rewards given to a set of the most prolific contributors. It finds significant positive effects on productivity for the top 1 per cent of contributors (judged by article edits) who had never before received such a reward. Yet, in a follow-up study seeking to widen the analysis to the top 10 per cent of most prolific contributors (Restivo and van de Rijt 2014), the authors find that the reward they hand out as an anonymous editor has no, or even negative, effects on productivity and retention.

To understand the potentially counterproductive effects of using monetary incentives to motivate volunteers, see Ariely et al. (2009), Bénabou and Tirole (2006), and Frey and Goette (1999).

On volunteer engagement and current trends in the third sector, see, for instance, Snyder and Omoto (2008) or Hustinx et al. (2010). Macduff (2005) coined the term 'episodic volunteer' to describe the observation that organizations have increasing difficulties retaining their members over longer periods of time. Several articles cover Wikipedia's struggle with declining retention rates among its contributors, especially among new ones. We recommend reading Halfaker et al. (2013), Suh et al. (2009), and Wikimedia (2011).

The important role played by awards in the voluntary and humanitarian sectors has also been noted by English (2005, pp. 58–9), who provides a partial list of the honours bestowed on Nelson Mandela to illustrate the sheer abundance of such awards. The author likens this to the spread of awards and prizes in the cultural sector.

We performed a survey among over two thousand voluntary organizations in the Swiss non-profit sector. This was done together with Anna Leisin (who wrote her Master's thesis about this) and is covered, among other studies, in Gallus and Frey (2016b). The results suggest that managers and directors of organizations in the non-profit sector consider awards to be important, but that only 38 per cent of the organizations make use of them. Our major take-away from the survey study is that information on the usefulness of awards to support the motivation and behaviour of volunteers is not yet sufficiently spread and integrated. Many organizations seem to be using awards, or at least to consider doing so, but there is limited information about what other organizations have been doing, and to what effect.

John List and co-authors have written extensively on field experiments, both about their own findings and about the methodology as such. This has given rise to a literature that has yielded path-breaking results. See, for instance, Harrison and List (2004), Levitt and List (2009), as well as List (2007, 2011).

6

Awards in Firms

Business and Other Private-Sector Awards

Practitioners in the private sector constantly witness the bestowal and celebration of awards, prizes, and medals (for empirical evidence see, e.g., Tise 2014). There are many company award bestowals that the public is not even aware of since the respective firms focus on publicizing them through company-internal communication channels, such as the intranet or company newsletter (see Table 6.1, Panel A). Other awards in the private sector transcend firm boundaries and are thus visible to company-outsiders and the general public as well (see Table 6.1, Panel B).

Consider the example of Steve Jobs to grasp the diversity of awards in the private sector. The founder and visionary boss of Apple, who became the symbol of an entire industry, received a large number of honours—from the state and public officials, from organizations in the non-profit sector, and from the business press. These include the National Medal of Technology given by President Reagan, the Jefferson Award for Public Service, and being named CEO of the Decade by *Fortune* magazine. The company itself, Apple, also directly honours its employees, for instance by giving them plaques and glass sculptures for the length of their service. This practice is emblematic for many other firms (see, e.g., the company illustrations in Gallus and Frey 2016a).

Employees are widely recognized as an important source for achieving and sustaining competitive advantage. Financial incentives have received most attention among the possible means for motivating employee performance, particularly among economists. However, a substantial body of research suggests that money may not always be successful in sustaining and raising employees' motivation (Frey 1997). When the use of money is perceived to be controlling, financial incentives may even backfire and undermine motivation. High-powered incentives can also lead to strategic behaviour, gaming, and costs arising from social comparisons and envy.

Table 6.1 Awards in the private sector

A. Different types of intra-firm awards

Primary purpose	Example
Employee motivation (actual and potential recipients)	*Employee of the Month*
Employee retention; recognition of loyalty	*Tenure-based awards*
Establishment of role models	*Safety awards*

B. Awards outside the boundaries of the firm

Primary purpose	Recipient	Giver	Example
Standard setting; Norm-establishment	Firm	Media; Non-profits; Public officials	CSR awards
Norm-establishment; Basking in reflected glory; Compensating local disadvantage (e.g. high tax)	Manager	State	National Medal of Technology
PR for recipient	Firm	Certifying organization	Stevie Awards
Attracting employees; PR for giver	Outsiders	Firm	L'Oréal–UNESCO Awards
Innovation	Outsiders	Firm	Inducement Prizes

Note: The different purposes are not mutually exclusive. For instance, the award Employee of the Month may also be employed to foster employee retention.

Using a field setting with paid workers, a recent experiment indicates that performance pay may have a negative impact on non-monetary motivations to perform well (Huffman and Bognanno 2015). This effect manifested itself only with a delay, and was not visible immediately. A survey shows that the majority of subjects in the treatment group found that the experience of performance pay made work 'less fun'. However, a sub-group of workers also reported positive psychological effects, suggesting that the impact of monetary pay on intrinsic motivation depends on personality factors as well as environmental conditions (e.g. for the public sector, see Delfgaauw and Dur 2008).

Many firms seem to be aware of the limitations of monetary incentives. They use non-financial rewards in an effort to sustain and raise employee motivation. Awards are a special kind of non-financial, yet extrinsic incentive, whose value resides primarily in the recognition conveyed among peers and in the public. An increasing number of organizations have developed award programmes as an important part of their human resource strategies (see the many examples of employee awards listed in Nelson 2012).

Awards provide a valuable means for motivating employees, but recent research has also shown that they can crowd out motivation and induce employees to game the programme. Employees not (yet) receiving awards may be envious and disturb the organizational processes. Research on awards given by outside organizations, such as the business press, more-over suggests that awards can motivate CEOs to extract higher compensation and engage in image-boosting activities such as writing books—at the expense of their firm's performance (Malmendier and Tate 2009).

It is not an easy task to design and implement an award programme that helps a firm obtain long-lasting competitive advantage. Managers using awards so far cannot base their decisions on a body of well-developed theory and empirical evidence. Rather, the scientifically based information is sketchy and restricted to selected cases (see Table 2.3 in Chapter 2). Some scholars (e.g. Gubler et al. 2016) adduce important evidence suggesting that recognition programmes can even backfire, e.g. when they reward the wrong persons and activities. Introducing an award system that is poorly designed not only produces a waste of resources; it can also have a significant negative impact on firm performance.

We first consider how awards create value by raising employee effort and motivation, and how this value can be captured through enhanced employee retention. There is an emerging body of empirical research dealing with the causal effects of awards on performance in the context of for-profit enterprises. We then look more deeply into how awards can destroy value when applied in firms. On that basis, we develop and propose a synthesis of the dimensions that seem critical for successful award bestowals. Finally, we indicate how the process of value creation and capture is contingent on the given firm's organizational characteristics and nature of production. A fuller analysis can be found in Gallus and Frey (2016a), on which this chapter is based.

Value Creation through Awards

Management can positively influence the behaviour of both recipients and non-recipients of awards. We argue that, under identifiable conditions, awards can enhance their recipients' intrinsic motivation and induce a crowding-in effect. They may also be used to create role models and subtly steer the behaviour of non-awarded employees.

Motivational Crowding-In

Intrinsic motivation is an important source of employee performance and it contributes to organizations' strategic competitive advantage, in particular where monitoring is costly and performance ambiguous. This applies, for instance, to extra-role behaviours such as helping out colleagues, but also to creative work and knowledge production. Rewards that come from outside and are perceived as controlling, as may be the case with variable performance pay, risk crowding out employees' intrinsic motivation for the incentivized activities. Symbolic awards are a type of extrinsic reward, yet they are non-material. We conjecture that, much like verbal reinforcements and tangible non-monetary rewards, awards are less likely than money to crowd out intrinsic motivation. We posit that they even have the potential to support it.

Research in psychology has shown that competence, autonomy, and relatedness enhance intrinsic motivation. Awards are well suited to cater to all three of them. When an award is handed out in a ceremony, the giver publicly recognizes the recipient's competence. The recipient's intrinsic motivation is publicized and supported, directing attention to the extraordinary achievements of the award winner.

Discretionary awards lend themselves most readily to rewarding employees without infringing on their perceived autonomy—they may even raise employees' sense of autonomy. These awards differ from contingent, ex ante incentives that are based on explicit criteria. Discretionary awards are given ex post, often as a surprise, and do not require performance to be meticulously defined and measured. Management can thereby recognize effort and performance more broadly. This is particularly valuable when it comes to recognizing and encouraging corporate citizenship behaviours, such as helpfulness and vigilance. Discretionary awards are less obtrusive than most other extrinsic rewards and therefore, as we argue, reduce the risk of crowding-out. Employees' perceived autonomy may be raised by the award givers if they signal support and recognition for the achievements. This can strengthen employees' relatedness to management and the organization, which further enhances intrinsic motivation.

As argued in Chapter 5, the symbolic content of awards may partly substitute for their actual material value (e.g. prize money). Purely symbolic awards allow creating value at low cost. A monetary prize, in contrast, may even dilute the signal of merit and put the winners' intent in question. Yet it must still be asked whether awards devoid of monetary benefits induce behavioural change in the context of the for-profit sector. Standard economics would be sceptical about such a claim.

Role Models

Management can use awards to celebrate and create role models, inducing non-awarded employees to emulate the desired behaviour. Where employees' expected contributions are difficult or even impossible to define, to identify, and to measure, it is strenuous to set ex ante incentives that induce employees to adopt the norms and behaviours required. In contrast, awards as an organization-level routine to celebrate exemplary behaviour help encourage and maintain a corporate culture that is built on these norms. The publicity of the award conferral serves to propagate what behaviour or work attitude management deems important.

The festive nature and the visual material documenting award ceremonies create a higher salience value for awards when compared to monetary compensation. In many, if not most firms, the income received is not revealed; employees are often explicitly forbidden to make it known to co-workers and outsiders. The size of the financial bonuses received can only indirectly be shown by lavish consumption expenditures. Employees may make an effort to indirectly reveal their high bonuses by spending much money on expensive houses and apartments, luxurious cars and yachts, fancy watches and jewellery, or costly holidays. While this conspicuous consumption may impress other people, it is never quite clear where the money came from. It may have been inherited, or it may have even come from some murky source, but it does not necessarily reflect the person's worthiness as a member of the firm. Awards, in contrast, make achievements visible and celebrate them in public. They help management to communicate a narrative that employees will remember. This can further increase the duration of the award's impact and spread management's message to more distant parts of the organization. But while these seem to be plausible effects, they still remain to be tested by field experimental research in firms.

Many award programmes seem to be designed to establish role models to motivate the workforce at large to adopt certain norms or to act according to the company's values. Companies such as Holcim, one of the world's leading suppliers of cement and aggregates, implement Safety Awards to encourage employees to pay heed to the company's Organizational Health and Safety guidelines. This goal would be difficult to communicate and enforce by handing out bonuses and other high-powered incentives. Such incentives would risk shifting the focus of the reward and making the desired behaviour appear purely instrumental. Awards, in contrast, draw attention to the importance of respecting the safety instructions. They also provide management an occasion to remind the entire workforce of the importance of safety throughout the year.

Unilever, a multinational consumer goods company, honours a highly select group of employees as Unilever's Heroes for having shown great passion, dedication, and initiative. The award programme aims to recognize and showcase individuals who have gone 'the extra mile', sharing their story on the global webpage so as to inspire others and to demonstrate the company's values. Employees can nominate their co-workers for an award, such as for Brave Actions, Fresh Thinking, Outstanding Commitment, or Passion and Drive. These awards are focused on employees' stories, and not on what employees receive if they behave in a certain way. It is the behaviour of award recipients that is central, not the reward. The labelling of the award winners as heroes clearly shows that the programme is aimed at creating role models.

Capturing the Value Created by Awards

For awards to generate sustainable competitive advantage, firms have to be able to capture the value created. They need to assure that the awarded employees will remain with the firm, instead of going on the market to achieve a pay increase.

Using Awards to Foster Employee Retention

Awards and honours have historically been used to create a bond of loyalty between the giver and the recipients, as we have pointed out in Chapter 2. This function of awards was well recognized by some of the major proponents of awards in history. For instance, Napoléon Bonaparte reportedly stated that the ribbons of an order tie more strongly than chains of gold.

When managers present awards to employees, they signal their intent to establish an implicit relational bond with them. This signal is stronger the more discretion is involved in the bestowal; it should therefore be stronger for discretionary rather than confirmatory awards.

On the employees' side, accepting an award signals approval of the organization's values and goals. The signal is projected outwards, e.g. towards colleagues, but the process may also entail self-signalling. We expect this self-signal of loyalty to be stronger the less money is involved in the award bestowal. For purely symbolic awards, recipients would find it more difficult to rationalize their acceptance of the award—it was certainly not done for the money.

The Risk of Value Destruction

Unintended Motivational Effects

Awards can also reduce the motivation of both recipients and non-awarded employees. For award recipients, awards can in principle have a dampening effect on their intrinsic motivation. We argue that this is particularly likely to happen when a substantial amount of money is added to the award, when it is seen as compensation rather than recognition, or when it is based on ex ante clearly determined criteria requiring a measurement of performance, as is mostly the case for confirmatory awards. Winners can then perceive the award to be controlling, which risks crowding out their intrinsic motivation.

Another unintended effect awards can have on their recipients is to foster overconfidence. The winners could then start to treat co-workers disrespectfully, or they may argue for a wage increase or accept an outside offer. These effects are particularly likely to arise when the prize money is substantial or when the same employee is awarded repeatedly.

Non-awarded employees may be demotivated through the award as well. If the award scheme only includes awards with high performance requirements, many employees may feel that they do not stand a chance of winning. These employees may give up altogether. We conjecture that confirmatory awards are more likely than discretionary awards to entail such effects because they confirm the existing performance hierarchy, giving accolades to the already established stars (e.g. the best salesperson) while neglecting less obvious candidates. Regular and relatively frequent award bestowals can partly mitigate this risk since they give others a chance to win the award in the future. They do run the risk, however, of inflating away the awards' value.

In Chapter 3, we presented a survey experiment using vignettes at an IBM Research Laboratory. The survey design made it possible to provide some insight into how people would likely react to being told whether or not they received an award. The results reveal that the motivation of winners is significantly higher than the motivation of losers.

In order to assess the overall profitability of an award scheme, the ex ante incentive effects of the awards on all employees need to be compared with the ex post impact on winners and non-recipients.

Gaming the System

Other potential risks of awards with explicit, pre-determined criteria include multitasking and strategic behaviour, where employees shift their focus on the performance dimensions relevant for winning the awards while neglecting other important tasks. Outright manipulation of the award programme is most likely to occur when clear performance criteria are coupled with considerable prize money or other highly valuable rewards, such as vacations. On the other hand, awards that accord their givers considerable discretion may invite influence activities, which equally destroy value. In these cases the award programme may severely hamper firm performance.

Social Comparison Costs

In a speech to the House of Commons in March 1944, Winston Churchill famously stated: 'a distinction is something, which everybody does not possess. If all have it, it is of less value.' An award needs to be kept scarce to remain valuable. Non-awarded employees, who are therefore in the majority, may react favourably and identify with the award recipient, or they may be envious and engage in retributive behaviours that harm firm performance. Several dimensions of awards determine their effect on non-winning employees. We argue that the risk of social comparison costs is the higher, the greater is the award's material value (prize purse), the less clearly the required performance can be specified and observed, and the more frequently the award is given to the same individuals. Confirmatory awards based on explicit and pre-specified criteria initially reduce the risk of social comparison costs. Over the long run, however, this advantage vanishes if the scheme produces a select group of repeat winners who always win the awards.

To mitigate the risk of social comparison costs companies may combine different award types, in particular, confirmatory and discretionary awards. This can allow them to spread the reach of the award programme without tarnishing the value of the individual awards due to inflationary use. Setting up an award scheme that includes awards that involve co-workers in the decision-making process as well as group awards may improve the perceived fairness of the programme.

Sustained Value Creation Must Consider Complementarities

The effectiveness of awards crucially depends on the particular firm's nature of production and organizational characteristics.

Nature of Production

Organizations relying on complex tasks where performance cannot be monitored or contracted and where outcomes are not readily discernible can leverage important complementarities with awards. Alternative incentives to awards, such as bonus pay, are difficult to apply under such conditions. This makes awards, and in particular discretionary awards, more important as a motivation instrument to generate value for the firm (see Gallus and Frey 2016a for more detail).

Firms can use award programmes more effectively if their production technology allows for a high degree of interaction between managers and employees. Greater interaction enhances managers' ability to make an informed selection of award recipients. Where managers can observe employees' general work input as a by-product of the work process, they need not tie awards to pre-determined criteria nor use potentially obtrusive instruments for assessing performance. A high degree of interaction allows managers to gain information about the employees' preferences and to personalize the awards, which should enhance their motivational and relational effects.

Where team production is prevalent, offering high-powered incentives for individuals can induce envy and shirking, and it is likely to hamper collaboration. Conditional on firm size, management may use group awards in such team production environments.

Firm Scope and Scale

Awards benefit from increasing organizational scope since a greater number of activities allows for a greater diversification of the award programme. Contrary to monetary incentives, award systems also benefit from organizational scale since this allows management to regularly bestow awards without inducing award inflation.

We expect larger firms and those with many activities to have more complex award schemes, requiring a higher degree of coordination among the different award bestowals and aggravating imitation for competitors. For smaller firms, regular bestowals risk either being taken for granted (due to the sense that the award has to be passed around) or entailing social comparison costs (because the set of non-recipients is clearly identifiable). These conjectures still need to be tested by empirical research; however, so far we are lacking comprehensive data on award bestowals across firms.

With increasing firm scope and scale, individual performance pay becomes less attractive while awards become more effective. In many contexts, we expect awards to be complementary to flat wages. Where firms are not able to offer workers their marginal product of labour because of excessive social comparison costs (e.g. due to envy), they may incentivize and recognize exceptional productivity by resorting to awards.

The IBM Corporation has a wide range of awards, including confirmatory and discretionary awards, some with large prize purses and others providing symbolic recognition and possibly a present. IBM's non-monetary awards allow its managers to recognize a wide range of activities, while its highly coveted IBM Fellowship award serves to motivate the top scientists.

The IBM Fellowship is a prime example of a company award that is of considerable strategic value for the firm. Its yearly bestowal is a company tradition that has been in place for more than fifty years and is hence difficult to imitate. The award's reputation greatly benefits from its former recipients, five of whom are Nobel Laureates. Thus, the company has leveraged its very specific resources in a way that allows it to incentivize top performers. Firms large in scale and scope have to strike a delicate balance between the incentives used for top performers and the remaining employees' wage equity concerns. By using awards to motivate top performers, IBM lessens this tension to some degree. Other employees may even take pride in belonging to the unit that has given rise to a superstar. To ensure value capture, the award is tied to an ambassadorship for winners, with the clearly communicated expectation that they further invest their effort in the company.

Conclusions

The emerging empirical literature on awards in firms suggests that awards can have a substantive positive effect on employee and firm performance, but that they may also destroy value. Successfully implementing awards is a non-trivial endeavour. There is no one-size-fits-all solution for how firms can implement effective award programmes. In this chapter, we propose conditions under which specific types of awards backfire. We also outline how firms can use awards to achieve a competitive advantage and safeguard the rents created.

Analytically, we can gain important insights from shifting the focus away from individual awards and towards entire award programmes—as we have tried to do in this and other chapters. This implies considering new issues, such as complementarities and substitution effects between different awards, and between awards and other incentives in place.

We discuss how awards can affect corporate performance, jointly with firm characteristics and resources, and why they are a valuable strategic resource. We also want to emphasize that there is a lot to be gained from more systematic data collection efforts, which will allow us to study awards and other incentives across different organizations.

Related Literature

This chapter is based on Gallus and Frey (2016a), where more references to the strategic management literature and to empirical evidence can be found.

Barney (1991) emphasizes the importance of employees as an essential resource for the sustained competitive advantage of firms. Frey (2005, 2006, 2007), Frey and Neckermann (2009), Neckermann (2009), and Gallus and Frey (2016b) discuss corresponding aspects of awards in the workplace. The important role of intrinsic motivation as a source of employee performance is discussed extensively in Weibel et al. (2010) and Osterloh and Frey (2000).

The possibility that awards may destroy value for the firm has rarely been discussed in the management literature. An important exception is Gubler et al. (2016), who find negative effects of an attendance award programme that was implemented at one of five industrial laundry plants in the United States.

Economic status models (relevant for awards as a positional good) have been explored, e.g. by Auriol and Renault (2008). The costs potentially arising to firms due to social comparison processes are studied by Larkin et al. (2012) and Nickerson and Zenger (2008), who focus on monetary incentives.

We only considered awards given within firms. That awards given by institutions outside the firm may destroy value for the organization is shown by Malmendier and Tate (2009), who find that awards given by the business press, such as Manager of the Year, can motivate CEOs to extract higher compensation. At the same time they were found to engage in self-image boosting activities at the expense of their firms' performance.

Empirical evidence on the value placed on awards by software salespeople is provided in Larkin (2011). Siming (2016) exploits a natural experiment and finds that even CEOs in the for-profit sector attach considerable value to symbolic awards. Neckermann and Frey (2013) and Neckermann et al. (2014) provide further empirical evidence for the case of an IBM Research office as well as for a credit card call centre.

Effects of role models on the behaviour of employees in firms are discussed by Coff and Kryscynski (2011).

In his book entitled *Obliquity: How Our Goals are Best Pursued Indirectly*, Sir John Kay (2010) shows how certain goals, such as earning prestige and admiration, are often missed when people directly strive to achieve them. This may also apply to status signalling through conspicuous consumption, which often fails to signal an individual's merits. In contrast, awards by their very nature make meritorious behaviour public. The recipients do not have to actively signal their underlying qualities. Signalling through awards will be the topic of Chapter 7.

7

Honours as Signals

Honours are by their very nature publicly bestowed in front of an audience. Publicness is a major source of value of these non-material tokens, and it sets honours apart from other rewards (e.g. bonus pay and praise). As we have shown in Chapter 5, even purely symbolic awards can be highly valued. To better understand why this is the case, it is important to study the signalling functions of awards, which are more varied than one might assume at first glance. We therefore aim to develop an understanding of the signals emitted when honours are given and accepted, and to highlight conditions under which signalling failures are likely to arise. We try to do so in a non-formal and engaging manner. Our comparative approach, contrasting awards with other motivators (and with monetary incentives in particular), allows us to distil some conditions under which decision-makers could more safely use other incentives than awards.

The framework in Figure 7.1 provides an overview of the different signalling episodes involved in award bestowals. The signaller (a single manager, committee, community, or organization) transmits signals by offering awards (instead of money, for instance) for certain types of behaviour. The selected award recipient (a person, group, or organization) also emits specific signals when accepting or, as is also possible, rejecting the award. The value of the award to its recipient usually exceeds the material costs that the giver incurs. This cost–benefit asymmetry is a great advantage of awards over other signals, such as bonuses, which often may not even be talked about with colleagues. The symbolic exchange between award giver and recipient moreover emits signals relating to the non-recipients of awards (e.g. other employees), and to the outside signalling environment of potential future employees, employers, and others. In line with Chapter 6 on award bestowals as a component of organizations' human resource strategies, this chapter also considers awards given within firms. We focus on the signalling

Stage 1: Award is presented

Signaller
Has underlying quality, intent, and beliefs (about employees and tasks)

Manager
Committee (group of managers and/or co-workers)
Community (all employees)

Signal receivers
Observe and interpret signals

Employees

Award recipient
Chooses to accept or reject award
Employee
Group of employees

Non-recipients

Outside signalling environment
Potential future employees
Potential future employers
Others

Stakeholders (e.g. investors, customers)
Social networks (family and friends of employees)
General public

Stage 2: Award is accepted or rejected

Signaller
Has underlying quality, intent, and beliefs (about employer)

Award recipient

Receivers
Observe and interpret signals

Manager
Other employees
Outside signalling environment

Figure 7.1 A framework of the signalling functions of honours
Source: Gallus and Frey (2017).

episodes arising when managers present awards that employees decide to accept or reject. There are of course also cases where employees give awards to each other or where entire organizations receive awards.

The Different Signalling Functions of Confirmatory and Discretionary Awards

As pointed out in Chapter 3, it is useful to distinguish between confirmatory and discretionary awards. Since confirmatory awards are tied to clearly defined and observable performance dimensions, they leave management little leeway to emit signals. In the case of the Best Salesperson award, for example, the person with the highest sales volume will almost automatically receive the award. Such awards mainly serve the award recipients to signal their quality—in particular, their abilities and motivation—to others inside and outside of the organization (e.g. potential future employers; see stage 2 in Figure 7.1). Managers can signal which behaviours are deemed important through the choice of the performance criteria that are relevant for winning confirmatory awards. Only changing the award criteria can give them some measure of discretion.

Discretionary awards, such as the Outstanding Employee Award, accord managers a higher degree of freedom as to when and for whom to use honours. These awards allow managers to emit stronger signals about their intent and quality. Discretionary awards transmit information that receivers can specifically attribute to the individual managers since they were under no obligation to give a specific award. In addition, the higher discretion enjoyed also raises signal costs, which increases the credibility of the signal.

There are two main sources of costs that we want to focus on. Both tend to be higher for discretionary awards than for confirmatory awards. First, managers typically have to invest more time and effort into the selection of candidates for discretionary awards. Confirmatory awards, in contrast, are automated and reflect the already established performance hierarchy (e.g. employee sales rankings). The second source of costs is the risk managers incur when actively deciding on whom to honour. As we will later discuss, signalling failure may arise, for example, when awards are given to undeserving employees. Any such failure will be directly attributed to the award givers and tends to harm their reputation (as well as that of the award they are bestowing). We expect a high risk of signalling failure (e.g. because it is near to impossible to judge the true quality of work) to induce managers to invest extra time and effort into the selection of candidates, which further increases the costs of such awards.

Given the higher costs of discretionary awards, using this type of honour may allow managers to emit stronger social signals than using confirmatory awards. Discretionary awards also differ strongly from signals that are normally sent by other incentives, e.g. by money that is promised for the fulfilment of pre-specified behaviours. As before, we therefore mostly focus on discretionary awards in this chapter.

Signals Emitted by the Award Giver

We focus on three channels through which managers can use awards as signals to indicate what behaviours they expect from employees. These channels help us understand why in some instances, managers bestow awards instead of monetary incentives or pure praise. The signalling channels are not mutually exclusive, but can be regarded as being complementary to one another.

Managers Signalling their Own Quality

Information problems can arise with respect to people's quality or their intent. In the case where a manager bestows awards upon employees, the awards transmit signals that will cause recipients, non-recipients, and the public at large to draw inferences about both the principal's quality and his or her intentions. If the signal is perceived as credible it will influence beliefs and may thus also alter the signal receivers' behaviour towards the managers, as well as the organization as a whole.

There are two dimensions of quality about which award givers convey information when using awards as signals: their skills and their authority.

By bestowing awards to honour exemplary behaviours (e.g. helpfulness), which are often not recognized by standard incentive schemes, managers signal their interpersonal skills to the award recipient, non-recipients, and the outside signalling environment. These skills include an ability and a willingness to attentively assess the effort and performance of employees, and to adequately appreciate them. The managers can reinforce this quality signal by the type of behaviour they choose to honour. Giving awards for pro-social behaviours signals the managers' attentiveness to social issues and interpersonal relations. Managers identified as being attentive, appreciative, and supportive of a positive interpersonal work environment are in a better position to foster a supportive work climate and to build social-exchange relationships with and among their employees.

At the same time, bestowing awards also signals the giver's standing as an established authority in the organizational hierarchy. Award givers must be in a position to confer prestige. In contrast to gift giving, awards are based on an existing hierarchy, which they reinforce. The award recipient cannot simply reciprocate the signal by offering an award to the superior.

The two signals of quality, interpersonal skills and authority, starkly differ from one another. Yet, we often see how they are skilfully combined in successful award bestowals.

Monetary incentives could, in principle, also be used to signal authority as well as social skills. However, it is more difficult to transmit moral or pro-social qualities in this manner because these qualities may conflict with the perceived nature of money. A friendly act undertaken by employees for intrinsic considerations loses at least partly its value when it is compensated for by money. While monetary incentives may be used to signal authoritativeness, they are less suitable for signalling interpersonal skills. They may even signal the opposite, for instance, when used to pay someone for having helped a colleague.

Signalling the Intent to Establish a Bond of Loyalty

Giving awards also allows managers to signal their own intent: namely, their willingness to enter a mutual bond of loyalty with the recipients of the award.

Two conditions are important for the award to be perceived as an authentic relational signal. First, the number of awards the giver bestows has to be limited since the quantity of awards is negatively correlated with the manager's perceived intent of commitment to a specific manager–employee relationship. (Similarly, a higher quantity of awards bestowed reduces their value as positional goods.) Second, the bestowal of awards has to be consistent with the other signals the award givers emit. For example, awards should not accompany a cut in salary lest they be perceived as cheap substitutes for adequate pay.

When recipients accept an award, this act signals to the general public that givers and recipients share similar goals and are loyal to one another. This is less the case for monetary rewards, not least because it generally remains unknown who received what bonus, and for what behaviour. Monetary incentives are less related to vague aspects such as loyalty and commitment to an organization—quite the contrary. It is, for instance, less likely to be considered immoral to work for an organization whose values and goals one does not share. What matters is that one has received sufficient compensation to perform the tasks. In other words: employees' readiness to work for an organization whose goals they do not share is compensated for in monetary terms. Conversely, there are many people who forgo a higher income to work for an organization whose values they share and are proud of. This is revealed, for instance, by the considerable number of well-trained graduates with degrees from famous law schools who choose to work for a humanitarian organization at a much lower salary than they could get at an established law firm.

When presenting awards to valuable employees, managers shift the relationship from a purely business-oriented interaction to a social one, which is based on shared values and goals.

Signalling Beliefs about Employees and Tasks

The choice of how to reward employees for outstanding behaviours signals the managers' beliefs about the types of employees (e.g. ability, motivation) in the organization. It also signals the managers' beliefs about how difficult or attractive a task is (Bénabou and Tirole 2003). Instead of offering high-powered monetary incentives, managers can offer attention or autonomy, and signal trust in the employee's motivation (see the discussion of Dur 2009 and Non 2012 at the end of this chapter). The decision to refrain from controlling behaviour through high-powered incentives and instead use awards to highlight outstanding examples ex post can reveal the managers' beliefs in the prevalence of intrinsically motivated employees.

Awards that signal the managers' trust and confidence in the employees' future performance can foster the latter's self-esteem and motivation. If used effectively, the manager positively recognizes the award recipient's intrinsic motivation (e.g. for pro-social behaviour) and may thereby strengthen that important form of motivation.

Observing the manager's choice to trust can lead other employees to infer that there is a sufficient share of 'well-inclined' employees in their organization, which may propel them to cooperate as well (e.g. by helping out others and exhibiting generalized reciprocity).

These signals of trust and cooperation can also influence the self-selection of employees into and out of the firm, thus altering the distribution of types in the organization. By illuminating pro-social behaviours, managers stand a chance to attract more mission-oriented, pro-social, and intrinsically motivated types, rather than employees who mainly care about their personal enrichment.

Discretionary awards allow managers to leave the targeted perform-ance sufficiently vague and only define it in general terms. They may even emphasize that the targets cannot be determined ex ante but that the tasks to be performed are left to the discretion of the award winners. Awards can, for instance, be given for helpfulness with no need to exactly define, measure, and enumerate the employee's single deeds. Thus, the less easily performance criteria and tasks can be defined ex ante and observed ex post, the more suitable we expect awards to be, compared to specific monetary bonuses. Under opaque conditions, awards still allow managers to influence their employees' behaviour by signalling what behaviour is cherished. In contrast, monetary rewards, particularly in their more stringent form of variable pay-for-performance, normally require sufficiently defined measures of performance. These aspects have been integrated into recent principal–agent theory (see, e.g., the survey on relational incentive contracts by Malcomson 2012). In particular, it has been taken into account that it is sometimes mistaken to just consider well-definable tasks and that this should be substituted for by a comprehensive evaluation of performance (e.g. Bolton et al. 2004; Daily et al. 2003).

Using signals rather than explicit performance contracts allows employers to signal their intent to abstain from control and instead grant autonomy. The managers thus signal that employees' intrinsic motivation is valued and that they are trusted. Intrinsic motivation, which as we argue can be supported by handing out awards, is a crucial prerequisite for creativity and extra-role behaviours, which are import-ant in many fields.

Signals Emitted by (Possible) Recipients

Awards also involve signals that are being sent by the recipients, usually when they accept and display the awards. These signals are directed towards the manager, whose offer to enter a relational bond is recipro-cated. They also have an effect on non-recipients and the public at large.

Employees Signalling their Own Quality

When accepting and displaying an award, agents emit different signals of quality towards various audiences. Employees accepting awards signal their membership in a group. An award's reputation crucially depends on the prestige of the group of past winners. This prestige has implications for the award recipients' social status. Their status vis-à-vis non-recipients is usually enhanced; although their status within the group of award recipients may be low, in particular if the award has several ranks and they have entered at the lower end of the status hierarchy.

Signals of Intent

Accepting an award signals the recipients' future intentions to align their behaviour to a certain extent with that of the giver. Otherwise, the award would have to be rejected. To the extent that award bestowals help to convey credible signals of bonding intentions and trust between management and employees, which the public nature of award bestowals normally reinforces, awards can reduce transaction costs. In this respect, awards are markedly different from monetary rewards and also from gifts. Accepting gifts carries a subtle obligation of repayment, which tends to result in a gift exchange. In the case of awards, however, the recipient can rarely repay the favour in the same currency (awards). The possibilities for reciprocation are channelled towards loyalty and respect. Moreover, monetary rewards and gifts are often privately conferred, such that there is no audience to attest and reinforce the mutual bond.

Signalling Failures and Unintended Consequences of Award Bestowals

We have discussed how awards can destroy value for firms in Chapter 6. Here, we focus on instances when awards have undesired consequences because their signal strength is insufficient, or because they send adverse signals. Chapter 8 provides a comprehensive discussion of the challenges involved in award bestowals.

The signals emitted by honours may be too weak to result in any behavioural change on the part of signal receivers. This can be the case if too many awards are bestowed, or if the signals emitted through the use of awards do not align with other signals managers send.

Awards are positional goods and derive part of their value from their rarity. When managers bestow more and more awards, these will at one point become meaningless. There may either be too many similar awards in circulation, or a given individual may have received too many similar awards.

Managers can counteract such award inflation by diversifying the awards used. They can resort to vertical diversification and use different ranks for a given award, such as bronze, silver, and gold; they can also horizontally diversify the award scheme by creating awards for different types of behaviours (Gallus 2011). Horizontal diversification in particular makes it difficult to compare the different awards. Ideally, every new award occupies its own mental bin (see Best 2011), such that it acquires and retains its special value for the recipient.

Signalling failures can also arise when managers send contradictory signals. This can be the case when managers behave contrary to the values upheld by the award, for instance. The prize money attached to some awards is another such source of signalling failures. It may be perceived as too high, overriding the honorific signal of the award, or too low, thereby challenging the seriousness of the award. What is seen as an adequate amount depends on the other monetary rewards used, and on the prize purse of other awards in place. In some instances, it may even be better to not attach any money to awards. This is the case, for instance, when the costs would be prohibitive, or when the value of the behaviour cannot be translated into numeric terms.

Signalling failures can also arise when undeserving individuals are honoured and when candidates publicly refuse to accept an award. We will discuss these cases in Chapter 8.

Conclusions

Managers can use the signalling functions of awards to subtly steer the behaviour of (present and future) employees, without having to recur to control through explicit, conditional incentives. However, the discussion of signalling failures also makes clear that awards have to be used with moderation, and that they can rarely be used as a substitute for money where money is already in place (e.g. to make up for a pay cut).

We argue that, in comparison to money, awards have a more sustainable effect on behaviour, particularly because their marginal utility decreases at a slower pace than does the marginal utility of monetary rewards. Awards also remain visible in the future, creating a trophy value that maintains the awards' salience and their signalling functions even over the medium and long term.

Related Literature

Over the past four decades, signalling theory has become part of game theory. It now spans various disciplines, extending from sociology to economics, management, political science, anthropology, and biology.

Gambetta (2009) provides an excellent survey of the different strands of the literature.

Gallus and Frey (2016a) served as a basis for this chapter. The distinction that information problems may arise either with respect to the quality or the intent of an agent is made in Stiglitz (2000, 2001). The central role of signalling costs in signalling theory is discussed in Bliege Bird and Smith (2005), Camerer (1988), and Riley (2001). The basic rationale, that these signalling costs often help separate true signallers from mimics who only pretend to possess the quality associated with the signal, has been introduced from theoretical biology, where the term 'handicap principle' was coined (Zahavi 1975).

Signalling plays a substantial role in management research. Connelly et al. (2011) review the management literature in which signalling theory occupies an important position. Suazo et al. (2009) use signalling theory to analyse the impact of human resource practices, such as performance appraisals or compensation, on the employee's psychological contract (Rousseau 1989). The importance of reputation in organizational contexts is shown, for example, in the reviews by Lange et al. (2011) and Weigelt and Camerer (1988), and in the studies done by Deephouse (2000) and Fombrun and Shanley (1990).

A more formal extension of our approach could usefully build upon and integrate the results from the economics literature on conditional altruism, which has its origins in Levine (1998) and was applied to the workplace by Robert Dur (2009) and Arjan Non (2012). Dur (2009) develops a signalling model in the spirit of Levine (1998), where managers differ in their altruism towards employees, while employees are conditionally altruistic towards the manager. The model shows that managers who offer low wages to signal that they instead devote attention to employees can better induce employees to stay at the firm and work hard than managers who pay high wages. The basic assumption is that employees are conditionally altruistic: they care more for their manager when they are convinced that the manager cares for them. Non (2012) also assumes conditionally altruistic workers as well as managers that are either egoistic or altruistic. He incorporates reciprocity in a principal–agent model to investigate the relation between monetary gift-exchange and incentive pay, while allowing for worker heterogeneity. Since some workers do not reciprocate the managers' altruism, the model shows that managers may find it optimal to write contracts that signal their altruism while screening reciprocal worker types. These contracts offer strong incentives and a high base salary.

Besley and Ghatak (2008) provide a most interesting analysis of positional goods as incentive devices within firms. They use a principal–agent model in which the principal (manager) can reward agents (employees) for good performance in conventional terms (i.e. with money) and/or by giving them a status good. The analysis shows how the firm can exploit a preference for status to create 'motivated agents' (in the sense of Besley and Ghatak 2005)—but only to the extent that the status good is valued, which depends on how scarce the reward is. The authors point out the need for a well-defined rule that ensures that only the deserving are rewarded (p. 206).

8

The Challenges of Using Awards

A Problem of Choice

Awards have many notable advantages over other motivators, but they also have their disadvantages. The benefits and costs of using awards must therefore be compared to those of other devices for fostering motivation, such as monetary bonuses, gifts, or simply verbal praise. In addition, it must be carefully considered what kind of award is most suitable under what conditions, and how the award can best be combined with alternative motivators. There are many different kinds of awards, and we expect that for some of them, the effects vastly differ. This still needs to be further explored by future empirical research. For a scientist, for instance, receiving an award from one's peers, from the media, from a non-profit organization, from a corporation, or from a government agency has a distinct personal value and emits different signals towards peers and outsiders.

Moreover, most awards have different ranks, or classes. As pointed out earlier in this book, this holds for all the European orders of merit modelled upon the example of the five-tiered French *Légion d'honneur*. Other orders have become even more stratified over time, such as the Order of Merit of the Federal Republic of Germany. This differentiation of the ranks of award schemes is observable in many countries and many sectors of society. In the United Kingdom, for instance, an MBE (Member of the Order of the British Empire) is on a vastly different level than a CBE (Commander of the Order of the British Empire). Interestingly, such differentiations are mainly recognized by actual or potential recipients of a particular award, who are astutely aware of even slightly higher or lower ranks. For instance, they are able to appreciate the (enormous) difference between the lowest British rank of knighthood (Kt, Knight Bachelor) and the highest Scottish rank of knighthood (KT, Knight of the Most Ancient and Most Noble Order of the Thistle).

In contrast, the general public cares little about these differences. The media are more interested in the basic fact that celebrities are given (or revoked) awards. Thus, it seems that Angelina Jolie's title Honorary Dame Commander of the Most Distinguished Order of St. Michael and St. George (in short, Honorary Dame), bequeathed in 2014 by Queen Elizabeth II, is not taken to be much different from being appointed a Lady of the Most Noble Order of the Garter, the United Kingdom's highest order of chivalry.

Award givers have to choose among many different sorts of awards. One is the distinction between confirmatory and discretionary awards made in Chapter 3. Among the recurrent themes is the question of whether to add money to the awards, how many awards to bestow, which communication channels to use to make the conferral public and reach the intended audiences, and whom to involve in the decision-making process. Although awards offer unique possibilities to achieve competitive advantage (Chapter 6) and emit signals about information that would otherwise be difficult to communicate (Chapter 7), an erroneous choice can cause substantial damage. This holds in particular for potential costs arising from social comparisons and envy by non-recipients.

To Give or Not to Give Prize Money

Many awards are accompanied by money. In the case of the Nobel Prizes, the prize purses amount to 8 million Swedish kronor per full Nobel Prize (730,000 British pounds, 850,000 euros, 950,000 US dollars, as of mid August 2016). Managers within organizations also often recur to a prize purse. A major reason for this choice may be that the monetary compensation going with the award is taken to be a sign that the firm takes the award seriously.

Not attaching any money to an award risks that the giver is perceived to be stingy. This risk is particularly relevant for award givers in organizations with high profits and liquidity, and in sectors focused on monetary matters, such as banking and other financial services. It should, however, be noted that monetary rewards in the form of compensation or bonuses may also produce effects that run against the giver's intentions. If the monetary sums are relatively high, employees may infer that the task must be uninteresting or particularly demanding given their skill set (an argument elegantly developed in Bénabou and Tirole 2003). Relatively low monetary pay, in contrast, may signal the giver's low appreciation for the task at hand.

In most instances, we argue, what greatly matters to recipients is the honour and recognition going with an award, rather than its direct monetary value. This has been illustrated with the natural field experiment at Wikipedia (Chapter 5). The results of other studies about awards suggest that this also holds true in the private sector (e.g. Larkin 2011).

The importance businesspeople accord to the recognition and status coming from state honours has been suggested by a study analysing the discontinuation of a state order (Siming 2016). In 1974 Sweden ceased giving orders of merit to its citizens for distinguished service. This decision was used as a natural experiment to establish the value CEOs placed on the forgone opportunity for symbolic distinction. When the orders were no longer bequeathed, the CEOs had to be compensated by higher monetary pay (with which they could engage in conspicuous consumption to signal their achievements). In this case the orders seemed to have served as substitutes for higher pay.

It is crucial for the value of awards that the givers make an effort to credibly signal their appreciation. Organizations in the voluntary sector may make a point of giving awards without any money attached in order to emphasize that they pursue different, and presumably more noble, goals than organizations in the for-profit sector (the choice may of course also partly be driven by the cash constraints these organizations frequently face). The same applies to a large number of award givers in the public sector. Thus, it would be considered improper if a recipient of the Most Noble Order of the Garter would also receive a considerable sum of money with the award.

Similar considerations apply to executives being appointed Manager of the Year. Receiving prize money together with this award could diminish its value if it interferes with the signal of merit. The intention behind the action being rewarded and lauded becomes less clear: is it the quest for personal enrichment or the desire to perform well, in the interest of the corporation and beyond, which drove the behaviour? Moreover, it is taken for granted that the recipients are wealthy due to the high incomes they most likely have earned in their corporate positions.

Award Inflation

Issuing an increasingly large number of awards undermines their value. Grade and title inflation are well-known and related phenomena. The bestowal of awards is only effective if their numbers are limited. When a particular award is handed out too liberally, recipients and the public may even ridicule it. The incentive and loyalty effects then become muted. Awards, generally, can suffer such a loss in value for two main reasons.

There can be too many similar awards in circulation in a particular community, such as a firm, an organization, a sector, or a country. This applies with respect to both awards and bonus payments, however. When awards and bonuses become a matter of course, they lose their additional motivating power. While awards can be differentiated to impede direct comparisons, money is one-dimensional and may lead to a vicious circle of ever increasing 'superstar' compensation. This may give rise to strong social inequalities and value destruction through conspicuous consumption.

A second reason why an increasing number of awards threatens their value lies at the individual level of the award recipient: if a single person has already received a great number of awards, the value of an additional award may be strongly diminished. Such decreasing marginal utility is more likely to hold for monetary rewards than for awards, however. There seems to be almost no limit to the number of awards people value. This was pointed out in Chapter 3 with the example of the First Duke of Wellington, who received a seemingly uncountable number of orders, decorations, and titles of nobility. But he certainly is no exception.

Decision-makers have various options to counteract award inflation within their organization. We have already introduced the two strategies of vertical and horizontal differentiation in Chapter 7. Instead of increasing the number of awards given at the same level, new ranks can be created (e.g. Knight, Officer, Grand Officer in the case of state orders). In addition, new awards can be created, which the recipients cherish. Such a strategy works if the new awards gain their reputation through the legitimacy that the giver enjoys. Monetary rewards, in contrast, are one-dimensional: they correspond to a particular sum of cash. The marginal value of money for a single person decreases the richer he or she is. It would, for instance, be difficult to induce Bill Gates to undertake any action by promising him money. In contrast, he might very well cherish receiving (yet) another highly valued honour.

We expect that the number of awards handed out depends on the giver's expected remaining time in power. Givers with a long future time horizon have an incentive to keep awards scarce. Shortly after coming to power, politicians or managers have an incentive to be restrictive in handing out awards because they would have to fully bear the costs of award inflation arising in the future. In contrast, if their time horizon is short, decision-makers are induced to hand out, and to create, a large number of awards. They only have to bear part of the future negative inflationary effects, so that the cost of producing more awards is low for them personally. This can indeed be observed for dictators before their fall. A pertinent example is Adolf Hitler, who in his last public appearance shortly before his suicide handed out the (formerly highly valued) Iron Cross even to children soldiers.

The same behaviour can also be observed for politicians in democracies before they leave office. Thus, British Prime Minister Harold Wilson created an excessively large number of (Labour) lords shortly before leaving his position. David Cameron distributed no fewer than forty-three so-called resignation awards. Among the recipients were persons considered to be rather undeserving, such as his family's retainers. Samantha Cameron doubtless valued the help of Isabel Spearman in picking fashionable clothes for public appearances, but many onlookers may have found it hard to see how that qualified Miss Spearman for the OBE (Order of the British Empire).

Such behaviour with respect to awards is similar to a political business cycle in fiscal policy measures in democracies. Its creation is motivated by the intent to maximize the probability of remaining in power. It follows that the cost of award inflation is smaller the lower the probability of re-election; hence, the higher is the expected number of awards handed out.

Well-known military decorations have become subject to inflation over the course of time. In the American Revolutionary War the Purple Heart was only awarded three times (Cowen 2000). In contrast, during the Second World War in one battle alone, at Iwo Jima, the United States suffered 28,686 casualties, each of which received a Purple Heart. The German Iron Cross, established in 1813, and highly esteemed up until the twentieth century, lost much of its lustre when it was given out to 5,400,000 soldiers in the First World War, in which 13.2 million German soldiers were engaged; on average, 40 per cent of all soldiers received one. As some soldiers received Iron Crosses of several classes, historians estimate that about 20 per cent of German soldiers were decorated in this way. Similarly, in the Second World War, 5 million Iron Crosses were awarded.

Award Failures

In some instances the intended goals of bestowing an award do not materialize. This may be due to unintended signalling effects (some of which were briefly introduced in Chapter 7), or to adverse effects on non-recipients' motivation and performance.

Inconsistent Messages

The effects of an award can be undermined if the givers emit contradictory signals, which put in question their intentions. An instance of such inconsistent communication arises if the givers themselves violate the values upheld by the award. If the givers are, for instance, generally disrespectful of others, and yet bestow awards to enlist others' helpfulness, the signal is likely to be ineffective. The prize money attached to some awards can also send confounding messages. The amount may be perceived as too high, thus overriding the honorific idea of the award, or too low, challenging the seriousness of the award.

The givers have to make use of awards in a diligent manner in order to convey the message as intended. This refers to the givers' own behaviour, as well as to the relationship between the award and other rewards.

Undeserving Recipients

Signalling failures also result from an erroneous choice of award recipients. Two cases need to be distinguished in this respect. Decision-makers may award a person while being well aware that the award recipient is not deserving of this honour. They may do so for strategic reasons, such as trying to bind the recipient to their cause.

Principals can also unknowingly bequeath awards to undeserving individuals. Such error can either happen because the givers are not aware that the recipients do not deserve the honour but rather mimicked the desirable behaviour, or because the award recipients behave in an undesirable manner after receiving the award.

When an award is given to a person known to be disloyal to the giver or to be pursuing incompatible activities, the giver's prestige is hampered. Erroneously honouring a person who then turns out to be undeserving similarly challenges the credibility of the award and the persons or organization issuing it, but the consequences are probably less grave.

To hedge against these risks, award givers tend to bequeath honours to uncontroversial individuals and organizations. In contrast, unconventional and unorthodox candidates may well be neglected because their behaviour is less predictable and therefore exposes the giver to greater risks. It has, for example, been rumoured that this was the reason why Gordon Tullock did not receive the Nobel Prize in Economics together with James Buchanan for their joint work in constitutional economics. The Nobel Foundation's decision-makers may have been uncertain whether Tullock would have behaved and spoken in the 'appropriate' way at the festive award ceremony and thereafter.

Award Rejections

When awards are offered to individuals who then publicly refuse to accept them the givers are put in an awkward situation. The value of the respective awards is reduced, as the potential recipients find it less worthwhile to have them. The more widely the refusal of an award is known, the greater is the damage to the reputation of the award, its givers, and past recipients. Most readers will probably already have examples in their minds where individuals turned down awards. A well-known case is French philosopher Jean-Paul Sartre, who in 1964 declined the Nobel Prize in Literature. Thomas Piketty, author of the best-selling book *Capital in the 21st Century*, provides a recent case in point, with his refusal to accept the *Légion d'honneur* in early 2015.

British honours have also been declined by a considerable number of persons, for quite different reasons. Box 8.1 provides a selection of names, among them many well-known ones. Such actions are particularly damaging to the monarchy and to the government, as they are often publicized in widely read newspapers.

It is quite possible that award rejections even draw more attention than award acceptances. Being in the limelight is particularly important for people in the cultural sector, in fashion, and in media, but perhaps less so for academics—except, maybe, if they intend to pursue a career as public intellectuals. We would hence expect more rejections in the cultural sector than in academia (holding all else constant).

The most important reason for rejecting state orders seems to be a fundamental opposition to the monarchic institution or to the ideology

---

Box 8.1 INDIVIDUALS HAVING DECLINED A BRITISH HONOUR (SELECTION)

Knighthood

David Bowie, Danny Boyle, John le Carré, Roald Dahl, David Hockney, Aldous Huxley, James Meade, J. B. Priestley

CBE (Commander of the Most Excellent Order of the British Empire)

Francis Bacon, J. G. Ballard, David Bowie, Albert Finney, Lucian Freud, Alfred Hitchcock, L. S. Lowry

Source: Wikipedia, 'Declining British Honours' (accessed 27 February 2017).

and policy of the government in power. But there are also other reasons. For instance, Sir Winston Churchill, KG, OM, CH, TD, PC, PC (Can), FRS, statesman and Prime Minister, declined the Dukedom of London being offered to him because he wanted to remain a member of the House of Commons.

There are cases in which individuals are forced to decline an honour, mostly by their own government. A famous instance is the Russian authorities forcing Boris Pasternak to decline the 1958 Nobel Prize in Literature. Such action tends to raise the award's reputation because the award's importance is underlined and the attention it receives is heightened.

When Bob Dylan was bequeathed the Nobel Prize in Literature in 2016, he reacted in yet another, novel way. For a considerable period, he simply ignored the fact and was not available for contact with the Nobel Prize Foundation. This behaviour must have greatly annoyed the members of the Committee because it suggested that Dylan did not pay much importance to this otherwise so much coveted prize. The instance risked to reduce the prestige of the Nobel Prize and to negatively affect the members of the Foundation and Committee.

In an effort to prevent refusals or disregard by potential recipients, many donors ask candidates in advance whether they would be willing to accept the honour. Where it is not possible to assure acceptance of the award, potential givers may find it beneficial to resort to more gradual and less official signals of appreciation, such as personal praise or invitations to give talks.

Attracting Competitors

Awards tend to reflect the recipients' latent qualities. When a person receives an award, the givers indicate that they value these qualities, such as work attitude or commitment. This, however, increases the outside options for the recipient. As has been discussed in Chapter 6, firms issuing an award to one of their employees for 'exceptional service' or achievement make it more likely that competing firms make an attractive offer to that employee. This risk can be mitigated by basing the award on criteria difficult to evaluate from outside. In the extreme, the award becomes a 'currency' that can only be used within the particular organization. Money, in contrast, is understood everywhere without ambiguity and, therefore, allows for comparisons of employees' performances across firms, raising the probability that the bonus recipients are lured away if they can communicate that information.

Controversial Award Names

Most awards carry a name referring to the sponsor—such as the Pulitzer Prize or the Albert Einstein World Award of Science—or to a person to be honoured, such as the Lawrence Oliver Awards, the Nansen Refugee Award, or the Gandhi Peace Prize. These names should be uncontroversial and illustrate a public acknowledgement of excellence. Alfred Nobel's name is not totally free of controversy, though, as the explosive invented by him is not only used for civil purposes but also in war. However, the hundreds of highly renowned recipients of 'his' prize, in particular of the Nobel Peace Prize, have helped overcome this shortcoming. There are instances in which this is not the case. A recent example is the *Theodor-Eschenburg-Preis* given by the German Society for Political Science (*Deutsche Vereinigung für Politische Wissenschaft*). The Prize was abolished after 2012 because Eschenburg was accused of having collaborated with the Nazis.

Negative Effects on Non-Recipients

By bestowing awards on only a select group of people, the giver runs the risk of affronting people who are not awarded. The danger of negative effects on third parties is higher in small, clearly delineated, and homogeneous groups of people. Where the reference group is established and interpersonal comparisons are thus induced, non-recipients can interpret the award as a signal of them not being considered meritorious, or as a signal of favouritism. Negative emotions, such as jealousy, and destructive behaviour, even sabotage, may result.

The research reported in Chapter 3 suggests that such negative reactions need not take place (Neckermann and Frey 2013). The reaction by non-recipients most likely depends on the way an award is presented and accepted, and on the possibility to receive awards in the future. If both the giver and the recipient make an effort to emphasize that the winner's success is also due to a collaborative effort, jealousy can be reduced. It is important to explicitly acknowledge that winning an award is normally due to the effort and performance of a whole group and is not only due to an isolated person.

Awards are often given to already famous individuals. Such bestowals draw attention to their engagement, such as helping children in developing countries. This may be a reason why Hollywood film stars are appointed Special Ambassadors by the United Nations. Such awards and titles reflect positively on other people engaged in similar activities, increasing the status of the activities and people involved.

The general public, which does not consider or aspire to getting a particular award, may be indifferent or may even take pride when others are honoured. This applies when generally popular individuals receive state honours, such as music stars (e.g. Mick Jagger being knighted), sports persons (e.g. David Beckham being appointed OBE, Officer of the Order of the British Empire), or movie actors and celebrities (e.g. Angelina Jolie being appointed Honorary Dame). The same applies when the donor signals a willingness to entertain closer ties with a particular part of the population by giving an award to one or several of its exponents. This was the case when the four Beatles were each awarded an MBE (Member of the Order of the British Empire) in 1965. However, at that time some former recipients of the Order were so offended by the decision that they sent back their own MBE to the Queen.

Conclusions

Donors are confronted with various difficulties when wanting to bestow awards. Honours must be kept scarce to remain valuable. The award givers must avoid inconsistent signals; their own behaviour must correspond to the message of the award. Adverse effects can be prevented by giving awards to truly deserving individuals, and not to people who might later act in a disloyal way. As honours signal to outsiders that the recipients are top performers, the danger that they are lured away by competitors arises. Managers can mitigate this danger by emphasizing the relational bonding function of awards and by communicating the recipients' implicit obligation to serve as role models for colleagues in the future. Yet, even loyalty is problematic when it leads to organizational blindness, hampering necessary change processes and ultimately reducing performance.

The fact that a given award has to be kept scarce and hence not everybody may receive it can cause serious problems. People expecting but not receiving an award may become envious or even resort to sabotage. However, they can also be induced to work hard when it is made clear that they can get an award in the future. Moreover, an award given to a particular person can be framed in a way honouring the whole group to which the recipient belongs. Another possibility is to include group awards in the recognition scheme. This makes losing less painful and gives lower-ability types the chance of also winning awards. Similarly, awards that are based on effort rather than outcomes can be used.

Related Literature

The number of awards givers hand out depends on their expected time in power, similar to the behaviour of politicians, which is at the basis of political business cycles. For the latter, see Mueller (1997, 2003). Gavrila et al. (2005) develop a model for managing the prestige of awards over time, taking into account the number of awards bequeathed. Best (2008), Tise (2014), and Nelson (2012) provide discussions of the phenomenon of prize proliferation.

Frey and Steiner (2011) explore a further example of award inflation, the title World Heritage Site, which has been accorded by UNESCO to more than one thousand cultural locations. The list was continually extended and now also includes environmental areas. In addition to sites, since 2008, UNESCO has moreover featured a Representative List of the Intangible Cultural Heritage of Humanity, which may potentially include thousands of non-material objects.

Cowen (2000) provides an extensive discussion of military decorations, in particular the American decoration Purple Heart. The damaging effect on motivation of handing out too many school awards is documented, for instance, in Kohn (1999).

The challenges involved in bestowing awards are still little studied. A discussion can be found in Gallus and Frey (2016a). The results in Gubler et al. (2016) warn of potentially negative effects (e.g. motivation crowding-out and strategic behaviour). However, the interviews by Neckermann et al. (2014) suggest that the reactions by non-winners of awards are rarely negative, at least if awards are bequeathed in an appropriate way. A recent study by Ammann et al. (2016) lends further empirical support to this conjecture. The authors analyse prestigious media awards given to CEOs and find that these awards have a positive overall welfare impact mainly because they induce the winning CEOs' competitors to higher performance.

9

What Do We Know?

Honours have many positive features that set them apart from other rewards, and in particular from monetary incentives. In this book, we have made an effort to illuminate these features and to show their relevance for the givers, recipients, non-recipients, and society as a whole. The following are some of the most important advantages arising from the use of orders, prizes, trophies, decorations, medals, badges, ribbons, titles, and other forms of honours.

Probably the greatest strength of honours is that they directly and succinctly cater to one of the major human desires: to be recognized and appreciated by others. This need seems to be innate to human beings, and it has probably existed since the beginnings of mankind. After all, humans are social animals. Awards serve this desire by explicitly naming and emphasizing the reasons why the recipients are honoured. The publicity surrounding the award ceremony strengthens the attention received by the award recipients. It also confers recognition upon the people involved in the decision-making behind the award bestowal (e.g. the individuals asked for nominations, the jury, the awards' sponsors), as well as, potentially, upon individuals engaged in similar activities.

Awards can raise the intrinsic motivation of their recipients because they explicitly commend them for their activities. Intrinsic motivation is a crucial element in many spheres of life, both in organizations and in society as a whole. Research in psychology has shown that competence, autonomy, and relatedness enhance intrinsic motivation. Awards are well suited to cater to all three aspects of intrinsic motivation. Intrinsically driven people are more creative and often perform better because they are interested in the task for its own sake.

Awards are particularly well suited to honour broad achievements and performance that is difficult to define and measure. This advantage becomes evident when individuals are honoured at the end of their professional careers. It is also relevant for early career awards, which are meant to signal potential without being able to guarantee that the expectations towards the recipient's performance will be met. In many cases, just giving money would be considered inappropriate both by the recipients and by co-workers, not least because it is extremely hard to evaluate and put a number on life performance or potential. Awards are specifically designed to be applied to performances that are vague but nevertheless of great importance. The congratulatory words at award ceremonies may overcome the inability to express the value of achievement or potential in numeric terms.

Awards are a personalized way to motivate people. They establish a bond of loyalty between the giver and the recipient, to be observed by both parties. This feature distinguishes awards strongly from monetary payments that do not entail any aspect of reciprocity above and beyond the contract closed. Following the market logic, a recipient of a monetary reward can without a problem turn to another firm or organization if a higher incentive is offered. Somebody performing a service for a particular political party for money could easily transfer his or her services to an opposing party without being criticized (much like mercenaries can switch allegiance in wars). In contrast, awards establish a special relationship between the parties involved. This has indeed historically been a major function of orders. The term itself originally referred to an order as a select group of men (such as the Benedictines or the Franciscans), rather than the wearable insignia most people nowadays associate with the term.

Relying on honours can also have some less fortunate consequences. Being cheap, awards may seduce givers to hand them out in too great a number. In this case, awards become ineffective or even the subject of ridicule. If the givers apply insufficient care in selecting award winners, the latter may turn out to be undeserving or they may later behave in an undesired way. The givers then are confronted with the consequential choice of either retracting the award or having to tolerate a person whose behaviour the givers disagree with. In both cases, the reputation of the award givers as well as of previous recipients is tarnished. Award givers also experience a loss of reputation if the chosen award candidate refuses to accept the honour or hands it back later in protest.

Donors must moreover take care to prevent social comparison costs from arising. Individuals who do not receive an award may become jealous and reduce their work effort, or, in more extreme cases, they may resort to sabotage. This is, of course, a problem that applies to all kinds of rewards, including to performance pay. However, while employees are admonished to keep the size of their bonus pay private, awards are bestowed in public. In order to mitigate possible feelings of envy the donors must make an effort to explain the reasons why a specific person is honoured. It may also help to emphasize the recipient's representative function, that his or her performance is the result of a collaborative effort, and not solely due to one person's isolated work. In addition, the donor can make clear that everyone has the chance of receiving an award in the future. If managers have a high ability in this regard, awarding a particular person may well induce non-winners to put in more effort in order to receive an award or another form of recognition in the future.

Prizes and honours of any sort should always be compared to other forms of motivating people. Among the most important forms are monetary rewards. It must be carefully analysed in what respects and under which conditions monetary incentives are superior or inferior to awards, and when the two forms of rewards can be usefully combined.

Monetary Incentives

Over the last decades, social relationships seem to have increasingly become ruled by incentives in the form of money. Variable performance pay has been widely introduced in the corporate sector to motivate people to exert more effort and work harder. Successful employees are promised higher bonuses if they reach or surpass goals that have been fixed in advance. In the corporate sector, a considerable share of employees' compensation is based on such flexible payment schemes; fixed income is in many countries less than half the total. Top incomes of the 'superstars' have virtually exploded and the income distribution has become distinctly more unequal.

The use of monetary rewards as incentives has been extended far beyond the market economy. In particular, it has been applied to the public sector and constitutes an important part of New Public Management, which suggests that public officials should be treated like employees in firms. Their income is made highly contingent on meeting or surpassing goals set for the future, although these are at times hard or even impossible to specify ex ante and to measure ex post. The same development has occurred in other areas of society as well. Thus, in some regions professors and other academics are paid according to how 'well' they publish, how often they get cited, and how much outside funding they attract. Sometimes students' evaluations of the scholar's teaching and supervising activities also enter the count. Similar incentive systems have been introduced in the health and hospital sector. Even some voluntary and religious organizations have followed this trend.

Monetary rewards have several well-known advantages over other incentives. Most importantly, money is a fungible good which allows the recipients to use it for whatever purpose yields them the highest utility. Money caters to the material desires of employees. Careful econometric research on happiness or subjective well-being has convincingly established that higher income raises people's happiness (see, e.g., Frey and Stutzer 2002a, 2002b).

Money is often a convenient instrument to motivate people because it is easy to understand, to handle, and to portion. It can be minutely adjusted to a well-defined task, which the superiors consider to have been performed in a satisfactory way. This is particularly the case when variable performance pay or bonus systems are applied. When money is handed out, the principals need not expend much additional thought or effort. In this sense, monetary rewards are undoubtedly efficient.

To incentivize employees with monetary bonuses is, however, also being met with heavy criticism. There are various important reasons why variable performance pay can be ill suited or even detrimental.

Monetary incentives risk crowding out intrinsic motivation. When external interventions are perceived as controlling by the people affected, the innate will to undertake an activity previously considered worthwhile for its own sake can be undermined. Performance pay can send the message to employees that money rules supreme, while the activity as such is less important. The activity is then reduced to its instrumental role in attaining the bonus.

Performance goals can be determined in a reasonable way for simple tasks. In today's developed world, however, there are few easy tasks remaining because machines and robots substitute for them. This tendency will be even stronger in the future when self-learning machines will take over many of today's jobs. We are already at a point where typical tasks require taking into account many considerations that are difficult or impossible to be determined well ex ante. This applies in particular to knowledge work, where it is rarely possible to fully describe and translate expectations into performance goals. As a consequence of setting incentives ex ante, employees may concentrate on meeting the performance goals, while disregarding other activities that may be crucial for an organization (the typical multitasking problem).

Another ramification of clear-cut performance criteria is that employees may be induced to actively manipulate the performance goals. When employees get a significant part of their income from meeting a number of performance criteria, they have a strong incentive to manage the level of achievement of these goals to their advantage. Activities are reformulated to meet the criteria, and thus to get the bonus. It has often been observed that managers of corporations are able to reach and surpass profit goals by 'cooking the books', or even by cheating (the Enron scandal is just one example). Consequently, the accounting figures published can be biased and then no longer reflect the financial conditions of the firm.

Another risk of aggressive monetary incentives is that employees start making an effort to manage the criteria themselves. This not only leads to excessive, undeserved pay for executives. It also has negative external effects on investors who are wrongly informed about the economic and financial state of a given firm. Similar observations can be made for other sectors in which variable performance pay has been applied. Doctors are induced to operate more, or to only accept relatively healthy patients when they are paid by performance instead of when they get a fixed salary, or are paid to maintain or improve the patients' health. The resulting unnecessary surgeries and misallocations create a heavy burden on patients and play havoc with the financial balance of the health system.

Econometric research on subjective well-being has shown that an increase in income is subject to diminishing marginal utility and tends to be short lived (e.g. Easterlin 1995, 2002). People do not evaluate their situation in an absolute way but have an inherent tendency to compare themselves on two dimensions. The first comparison dimension is time. People get used to ever increasing incomes. They adapt to higher incomes so that their happiness tends to revert to the level attained in the past. This adaptation is not complete but nevertheless significant.

The second dimension of comparisons is social. People compare their own income position to that of others. The relevant reference group consists above all of friends, relatives, neighbours, and work colleagues. It follows that while income is of great importance at a low level of material well-being, once a higher income is achieved, other determinants become more relevant. One of them is esteem and the recognition coming from others, in particular from one's peer group, family, and friends.

Given the developments outlined here, we expect honours to become even more important in the future than they already are at present.

In Need of a Comparative Perspective

These negative features of using money to induce better performance do not mean that variable performance pay can or should never be used. But much care must be taken not to overdo its application. In particular, monetary incentives should not be used as the one and only means for motivating people and recognizing achievement. Our book suggests that awards in many cases are uniquely suited to induce people to act in the interest of the givers. We have argued that this is likely to be the case when the main goal of an award is to provide the recipients with recognition and appreciation, when intrinsic motivation needs to be maintained or strengthened, when the task is vague and the way it has to be fulfilled must to some extent be left to the employees, and when it is important that both the givers and the recipients be bound by mutual bonds of loyalty.

Monetary rewards are appropriate when the recipients need more material resources to lead a good life, and when a large number of people are involved so that the incentive system has to be simple and straightforward to apply. Monetary incentives are crucial for tasks that people are not intrinsically motivated to fulfil.

In some cases the advantages of awards can be combined with monetary rewards. Adding a monetary prize to awards may serve givers to signal that the goals expressed by the awards are important to them and deserve special attention. Adding prize money serves to establish the awards' value to outside observers and may provide an additional extrinsic motivation for employees to raise their performance. A similar effect is achieved by attaching gifts or other privileges to awards.

Yet, the effects of the two motivators cannot simply be added under all circumstances. Monetary checks that are added to some awards may undermine the intrinsic and image motivations of the award recipients. Social comparison processes between recipients and non-recipients may result in value destruction. We posit that using purely symbolic awards reduces these risks while also lowering costs. Such awards are moreover better suited for creating role models since the signal of merit is not tarnished by money. However, not all organizations are able to forgo money as a source of value for their awards. This is only possible if they manage to sufficiently substitute the monetary prize by symbolic content.

Conclusions and Open Issues

The Economics of Awards is still in its beginnings. Further progress must and can be made in the future in various areas. We will discuss some of them to conclude our book.

Comprehensive and reliable data on awards are scarce. While there is some information available on particular honours, especially those handed out by some monarchs or states in the past, the research on honours would benefit tremendously from a database of internationally comparable data on awards in different sectors and organizations.

There is still little information on which persons receive awards, and for what. The literature on particular honours, especially on state orders and decorations, extensively lists the legal aspects of award bestowals, but it rarely notes the exact reasons why people are honoured. While this information seems to be rather straightforward for confirmatory awards, it is by their very nature difficult to identify for discretionary awards. The respective information in most cases is not made public by the award-giving organizations.

Little is known about which individuals and groups do not get awards, what type of performance is disregarded, and what the non-winners' reactions are. In Chapters 6 and 8 we have noted some preliminary evidence in this regard. Envy and other negative consequences of social comparison processes can lead to destructive behaviours. This needs to be analysed in more depth in the future to better understand the conditions under which certain types of awards and other non-financial incentives destroy rather than create value.

More should be known about why some organizations hand out awards while others do not. It should be more fully studied what benefits organizations derive from bequeathing awards, above and beyond providing incentives at low cost, securing recipients' loyalty, providing a networking occasion, standing in the limelight, and basking in the glory of award recipients.

Broader knowledge is needed about the effects of awards, ex ante (on the people striving to receive them) and ex post (subsequent to their bestowal). Various dimensions need to be considered. Awards may be accompanied by vastly different sizes of present or future material benefits. For some awards there may be no material implications at all, and the benefit lies entirely in the recognition and prestige gained. For other awards, the income effect enjoyed by the recipients may be substantial. The fundamental causality issue identified in Chapters 4 and 5 arises. Winning an award may lead to higher future income, but the higher future income might have also occurred without getting the award, simply because award recipients are especially gifted individuals.

In general, the Economics of Awards would benefit from a clearer understanding of how the motivational effects of awards are shaped by specific design choices pertaining to the award scheme as a whole (e.g. what behaviours to honour, how many people to give awards to, which awards to combine), as well as by the interactions of awards with other rewards. This will also depend on the conditions surrounding the award bestowal, some of which have been discussed in Chapter 6. Further advancing this line of research will allow us to gain deeper insights into the conditions under which awards should and should *not* be used.

As these points illustrate, the Economics of Awards is faced with a number of open issues and there are many intriguing questions to be addressed by future research.

Related Literature

For a critical perspective on the trend towards pay-for-performance, see Bebchuk and Fried (2004) and Frey and Osterloh (2012).

Surveys of the major results in Happiness Research are provided in Dolan et al. (2008), Frey (2008), Frey and Stutzer (2002a, 2002b), and Layard (2011). Stutzer (2004) draws attention to the importance of income aspirations, rather than absolute income and consumption levels.

Monetary incentives and awards are not the sole rewards potentially suffering from inflation. The value of praise, for instance, also diminishes when it is used too liberally (see, e.g., Kohn 1999).

References

Abadie, Alberto and Gardeazabal, Javier. 2003. 'The Economic Costs of Conflict: A Case Study of the Basque Country'. *American Economic Review* 93: 113–32.

Akerlof, George A. and Kranton, Rachel E. 2000. 'Economics and Identity'. *Quarterly Journal of Economics* 115: 715–53.

Akerlof, George A. and Kranton, Rachel E. 2005. 'Identity and the Economics of Organisations'. *Journal of Economic Perspectives* 19: 9–32.

Allen, Michael Patrick and Parsons, Nicholas L. 2006. 'The Institutionalization of Fame: Achievement, Recognition, and Cultural Consecration in Baseball'. *American Sociological Review* 71: 808–25.

Ammann, Manuel, Horsch, Philipp, and Oesch, David. 2016. 'Competing with Superstars'. *Management Science* 62: 2842–58.

Anand, Narasimhan and Jones, Brittany C. 2008. 'Tournament Rituals, Category Dynamics, and Field Configuration: The Case of the Booker Prize'. *Journal of Management Studies* 45: 1036–60.

Anand, Narasimhan and Watson, Mary R. 2004. 'Tournament Rituals in the Evolution of Fields: The Case of the Grammy Awards'. *Academy of Management Journal* 47: 59–80.

Ariely, Dan. 2016. *Payoff: The Hidden Logic that Shapes Our Motivations*. New York: TEDBooks.

Ariely, Dan, Bracha, Anat, and Meier, Stephan. 2009. 'Doing Good or Doing Well? Image Motivation and Monetary Incentives in Behaving Prosocially'. *American Economic Review* 99: 544–55.

Ashraf, Nava, Bandiera, Oriana, and Kelsey, Jack B. 2014. 'No Margin, No Mission? A Field Experiment on Incentives for Public Service Delivery'. *Journal of Public Economics* 120: 1–17.

Auriol, Emmanuelle and Renault, Régis. 2008. 'Status and Incentives'. *RAND Journal of Economics* 39: 305–26.

Azoulay, Pierre, Stuart, Toby, and Wang, Yanbo. 2013. 'Matthew: Effect or Fable?' *Management Science* 60: 92–109.

Baker, George P. 1992. 'Incentive Contracts and Performance Measurement'. *Journal of Political Economy* 100: 598–614.

Balzan Foundation. 2012. *The Balzan Prizewinners' Research Projects: An Overview 2012*. Milano: International Balzan Foundation.

Bandiera, Oriana, Larcinese, Valentino, and Rasul, Imran. 2009. 'Blissful Ignorance? Evidence from a Natural Experiment on the Effect of Individual Feedback on Performance'. *Policy Research Working Paper Series*.

Bannier, Christina E., Feess, Eberhard, and Packham, Natalie. 2013. 'Incentive Schemes, Private Information and the Double-Edged Role of Competition for Agents'. Mimeo London School of Economics.

Barney, Jay B. 1991. 'Firm Resources and Sustained Competitive Advantage'. *Journal of Management* 17: 99–120.

Barro, Robert J., McCleary, Rachel M., and McQuoid, Alexander. 2011. 'Economics of Sainthood (a Preliminary Investigation)'. In *The Oxford Handbook of the Economics of Religion*, Mccleary, Rachel M. (ed.). Oxford, UK: Oxford University Press, 191–216.

Bebchuk, Lucian A. and Fried, Jesse M. 2004. *Pay without Performance: The Unfulfilled Promise of Executive Compensation*. Cambridge, MA: Harvard University Press.

Bénabou, Roland and Tirole, Jean. 2003. 'Intrinsic and Extrinsic Motivation'. *Review of Economic Studies* 70: 489–520.

Bénabou, Roland and Tirole, Jean. 2006. 'Incentives and Prosocial Behaviour'. *American Economic Review* 96: 1652–78.

Bénabou, Roland and Tirole, Jean. 2016. 'Bonus Culture: Competitive Pay, Screening, and Multitasking'. *Journal of Political Economy* 124: 305–70.

Bertrand, Marianne and Mullainathan, Sendhil. 2001. 'Do People Mean What they Say? Implications for Subjective Survey Data'. *American Economic Review, Papers, and Proceedings* 91: 67–72.

Besley, Timothy. 2005. 'Notes on Honours'. *Mimeo London School of Economics*, unpublished paper.

Besley, Timothy and Ghatak, Maitreesh. 2005. 'Competition and Incentives with Motivated Agents'. *American Economic Review* 95: 616–36.

Besley, Timothy and Ghatak, Maitreesh. 2008. 'Status Incentives'. *American Economic Review* 98: 206–11.

Best, Joel. 2008. 'Prize Proliferation'. *Sociological Forum* 23: 1–27.

Best, Joel. 2011. *Everyone's a Winner. Life in the Congratulatory Culture*. Berkeley: University of California Press.

Blanes i Vidal, Jordi and Nossol, Mareike. 2011. 'Tournaments without Prizes: Evidence from Personnel Records'. *Management Science* 57: 1721–36.

Bliege Bird, Rebecca and Smith, Eric Alden. 2005. 'Signaling Theory, Strategic Interaction, and Symbolic Capital'. *Current Anthropology* 46: 221–48.

Bolton, Gary E., Katok, Elena, and Ockenfels, Axel. 2004. 'How Effective Are Electronic Reputation Mechanisms? An Experimental Investigation'. *Management Science* 50: 1587–602.

Bolton, Gary E., Greiner, Ben, and Ockenfels, Axel. 2013. 'Engineering Trust: Reciprocity in the Production of Reputation Information'. *Management Science* 59: 265–85.

Borjas, George J. and Doran, Kirk B. 2015. 'Prizes and Productivity: How Winning the Fields Medal Affects Scientific Output'. *Journal of Human Resources* 50: 728–58.

Bowles, Samuel. 2008. 'Policies Designed for Self-Interested Citizens May Undermine "the Moral Sentiments": Evidence from Economic Experiments'. *Science* 320: 1605–9.

Bowles, Samuel. 2009. 'When Economic Incentives Backfire'. *Harvard Business Review* 87: 22–3.

Bowles, Samuel and Polania-Reyes, Sandra. 2012. 'Economic Incentives and Social Preferences: Substitutes or Complements?' *Journal of Economic Literature* 50: 368–425.

Bradler, Christiane, Dur, Robert, Neckermann, Susanne, and Non, Arjan. 2016. 'Employee Recognition and Performance: A Field Experiment'. *Management Science* 62: 3085–99.

Brennan, Geoffrey and Pettit, Philip. 2004. *The Economy of Esteem: An Essay on Civil and Political Society.* Oxford, UK: Oxford University Press.

Bruni, Luigino. 2013. 'On Virtues and Awards: Giacinto Dragonetti and the Tradition of Economia Civile in Enlightenment Italy'. *Journal of the History of Economic Thought* 35: 517–35.

Brunt, Liam, Lerner, Josh, and Nicholas, Tom. 2012. 'Inducement Prizes and Innovation'. *Journal of Industrial Economics* 60: 657–96.

Cabinet Office. 2016. 'The Queen's Birthday Honours 2016'. 10 June. https://www.gov.uk/government/news/the-queens-birthday-honours-2016 (accessed 27 February 2017).

Camerer, Colin. 1988. 'Gifts as Economic Signals and Social Symbols'. *American Journal of Sociology* 94: S180–S214.

Carey, Catherine. 2008. 'Modeling Collecting Behaviour: The Role of Set Completion'. *Journal of Economic Psychology* 29: 336–47.

Chan, Ho Fai and Torgler, Benno. 2012. 'Econometric Fellows and Nobel Laureates in Economics'. *Economics Bulletin* 32: 3365–77.

Chan, Ho Fai, Frey, Bruno S., Gallus, Jana, Schaffner, Markus, Torgler, Benno, and Whyte, Stephen. 2014. 'Do the Best Scholars Attract the Highest Speaking Fees? An Exploration of Internal and External Influence'. *Scientometrics* 101: 793–817.

Chan, Ho Fai, Frey, Bruno S., Gallus, Jana, and Torgler, Benno. 2014. 'Academic Honors and Performance'. *Labour Economics* 31: 188–204.

Chan, Ho Fai, Frey, Bruno S., Gallus, Jana, Schaffner Markus, Torgler, Benno, and Whyte, Stephen. 2015. 'External Influence as an Indicator of Scholarly Importance?' *CESifo Economic Studies* 62: 170–95.

Coff, Russell W. and Kryscynski, David. 2011. 'Drilling for Micro-Foundations of Human Capital-Based Competitive Advantages'. *Journal of Management* 37: 1429–43.

Connelly, Brian L., Certo, S. Trevis, Ireland, R. Duane, and Reutzel, Christopher R. 2011. 'Signaling Theory: A Review and Assessment'. *Journal of Management* 37: 39–67.

Cowen, Tyler. 2000. *What Price Fame?* Cambridge, MA; London, England: Harvard University Press.

Crawford, Elisabeth. 1987. *The Beginnings of the Nobel Institution: The Science Prizes, 1901–1915.* Cambridge, UK: Cambridge University Press.

Csikszentmihalyi, Mihaly. 1997. *Flow and the Psychology of Discovery and Invention.* New York: Harper Perennial.

Curie, Eve. 1938. *Madame Curie*. Paris: Gallimard.

Daily, Catherine, Dalton, Dan, and Cannella, Albert. 2003. 'Corporate Governance: Decades of Dialogue and Data'. *Academy of Management Review* 28: 371–82.

Deci, Edward L. 1971. 'Effects of Externally Mediated Rewards on Intrinsic Motivation'. *Journal of Personality and Social Psychology* 18: 105–15.

Deci, Edward L. 1975. *Intrinsic Motivation*. New York: Plenum Press.

Deci, Edward L. and Ryan, Richard M. 1985. *Intrinsic Motivation and Self-Determination in Human Behaviour*. New York: Plenum Press.

Deephouse, David L. 2000. 'Media Reputation as a Strategic Resource: An Integration of Mass Communication and Resource-Based Theories'. *Journal of Management* 26: 1091–112.

Delfgaauw, Josse and Dur, Robert. 2008. 'Incentives and Workers' Motivation in the Public Sector'. *Economic Journal* 118: 171–91.

Delmonico, Francis L., Arnold, Robert, Scheper-Hughes, Nancy, Siminoff, Laura A., Kahn, Jeffrey, and Youngner, Stuart J. 2002. 'Ethical Incentives—Not Payment—for Organ Donation'. *New England Journal of Medicine* 346: 2002–5.

Dolan, Paul, Peasgood, Tessa, and White, Mathew. 2008. 'Do We Really Know What Makes Us Happy? A Review of the Economic Literature on the Factors Associated with Subjective Well-Being'. *Journal of Economic Psychology* 29: 94–122.

Duckers, Peter. 2004. *British Orders and Decorations*. Buckinghamshire, UK: Shire Publications.

Dur, Robert. 2009. 'Gift Exchange in the Workplace: Money or Attention?' *Journal of the European Economic Association* 7: 550–60.

Easterlin, Richard. 1995. 'Will Raising Incomes of All Increase the Happiness of All?' *Journal of Economic Behaviour and Organisation* 14: 35–48.

Easterlin, Richard. 2002. *Happiness in Economics*. Cheltenham, UK; Northampton, MA: Edward Elgar Publishing.

Economist, The. 2004. 'Titles. Honour Killings. A Ridiculous, Outdated System that Cannot be Improved Upon'. 15 July.

Ellingsen, Tore and Johannesson, Magnus. 2008. 'Pride and Prejudice: The Human Side of Incentive Theory'. *American Economic Review* 98: 990–1008.

English, James F. 2005. *The Economy of Prestige: Prizes, Awards, and the Circulation of Cultural Value*. Cambridge, MA: Harvard University Press.

English, James F. 2014. 'The Economics of Cultural Awards'. In *The Handbook of the Economics of Art and Culture (Vol. 2)*, Ginsburgh, Victor A. and Throsby, David (eds). Amsterdam: Elsevier, 119–43.

Evers, Ellen R. K., Zeelenberg, Marcel, and Inbar, Yoel. 2016. 'The Set-Completion Premium'. Unpublished working paper.

Fehr, Ernst and Schmidt, Klaus M. 2004. 'Fairness and Incentives in a Multi-Task Principal–Agent Model'. *Scandinavian Journal of Economics* 106: 453–74.

Feldman, Burton. 2001. *The Nobel Prize: A History of Genius, Controversy, and Prestige*. New York: Arcade Publishing.

Fombrun, Charles and Shanley, Mark. 1990. 'What's in a Name? Reputation Building and Corporate Strategy'. *Academy of Management Journal* 33: 233–58.

Frank, Robert H. 1985. *Choosing the Right Pond: Human Behaviour and the Quest for Status*. New York: Oxford University Press.

Frey, Bruno S. 1992. 'Tertium Datur: Pricing, Regulating and Intrinsic Motivation'. *Kyklos* 45: 161–84.

Frey, Bruno S. 1997. *Not Just For the Money: An Economic Theory of Personal Motivation*. Cheltenham/Brookfield: Edward Elgar Publishing.

Frey, Bruno S. 2005. 'Knight Fever: Towards an Economics of Awards'. *CESifo Working Paper No. 1468*: http://www.econstor.eu/handle/10419/18832 (accessed 17 May 2013).

Frey, Bruno S. 2006. 'Giving and Receiving Awards'. *Perspectives on Psychological Science* 1: 377–88.

Frey, Bruno S. 2007. 'Awards as Compensation'. *European Management Review* 4: 6–14.

Frey, Bruno S. 2008. *Happiness: A Revolution in Economics*. Cambridge, MA: MIT Press.

Frey, Bruno S. and Gallus, Jana. 2014. 'The Power of Awards'. *The Economists' Voice* 11: 1–5.

Frey, Bruno S. and Goette, Lorenz. 1999. *Does Pay Motivate Volunteers?* Zurich: Institute for Empirical Research in Economics, University of Zurich.

Frey, Bruno S. and Jegen, Reto. 2001. 'Motivation Crowding Theory'. *Journal of Economic Surveys* 15: 589–611.

Frey, Bruno S. and Neckermann, Susanne. 2009. 'Awards: A View from Economics'. In *The Economics of Ethics and the Ethics of Economics*, Brennan, Geoffrey and Eusepi, Giuseppe (eds). Cheltenham, UK; Northampton, MA: Edward Elgar Publishing, 73–88.

Frey, Bruno S. and Osterloh, Margit. 2012. 'Stop Tying Pay to Performance'. *Harvard Business Review* 90: 1404–4.

Frey, Bruno S. and Steiner, Lasse. 2011. 'World Heritage List: Does it Make Sense?' *International Journal of Cultural Policy* 17: 555–73.

Frey, Bruno S. and Stutzer, Alois. 2002a. 'What can Economists Learn from Happiness Research?' *Journal of Economic Literature* 40: 402–35.

Frey, Bruno S. and Stutzer, Alois. 2002b. *Happiness and Economics: How the Economy and Institutions Affect Human Well-Being*. Princeton, NJ: Princeton University Press.

Galloway, Peter. 2002. *The Order of St. Michael and St. George*. Lingfield: Third Millennium.

Gallus, Jana. 2011. 'The Economics of Awards'. Master's thesis, University of St. Gallen.

Gallus, Jana. 2016. 'Fostering Public Good Contributions with Symbolic Awards: A Large-Scale Natural Field Experiment at Wikipedia'. *Management Science*. http://dx.doi.org/10.1287/mnsc.2016.2540 (accessed 27 February 2017).

Gallus, Jana and Frey, Bruno S. 2016a. 'Awards: A Strategic Management Perspective'. *Strategic Management Journal* 37: 1699–714.

Gallus, Jana and Frey, Bruno S. 2016b. 'Awards as Non-Monetary Incentives'. *Evidence-Based HRM* 4: 81–91.

Gallus, Jana and Frey, Bruno S. 2017. 'Awards as Strategic Signals'. *Journal of Management Inquiry* 26: 76–85.

Gambetta, Diego. 2009. 'Signaling'. In *The Oxford Handbook of Analytical Sociology*, Hedstrom, Peter and Bearman, Peter (eds). Oxford: Oxford University Press, 168–94.

Gavrila, Caius, Caulkins, Jonathan P., Feichtinger, Gustav, Tragler, Gernot, and Hartl, Richard F. 2005. 'Managing the Reputation of an Award to Motivate Performance'. *Mathematical Methods of Operations Research* 61: 1–22.

German Socio-Economic Panel. 2016. Deutsches Institut für Wirtschaftsforschung DIW, Berlin.

Gigerenzer, Gerd. 2014. *Risk Savvy: How to Make Good Decisions*. New York: Penguin.

Ginsburgh, Victor A. and van Ours, Jan C. 2003. 'Expert Opinion and Compensation: Evidence from a Musical Competition'. *American Economic Review* 93: 289–96.

Ginsburgh, Victor and Weyers, Sheila. 2014. 'Nominees, Winners, and Losers'. *Journal of Cultural Economics* 38: 291–313.

Gneezy, Uri, Meier, Stephan, and Rey-Biel, Pedro. 2011. 'When and Why Incentives (Don't) Work to Modify Behavior'. *Journal of Economic Perspectives* 25: 191–210.

Grant, Ruth W. 2011. *Strings Attached: Untangling the Ethics of Incentives*. Princeton, NJ: Princeton University Press.

Gubler, Timothy, Larkin, Ian, and Pierce, Lamar. 2016. 'Motivational Spillovers from Awards: Crowding Out in a Multitasking Environment'. *Organisation Science* 27: 286–303.

Halfaker, Aaron, Keyes, Oliver, and Taraborelli, Dario. 2013. 'Making Peripheral Participation Legitimate: Reader Engagement Experiments in Wikipedia'. *Proceedings of the 2013 Conference on Computer-Supported Cooperative Work*. ACM: 849–60. doi:10.1145/2441776.2441841 (accessed 27 February 2017).

Hamermesh, Daniel S. and Schmidt, Peter. 2003. 'The Determinants of Econometric Society Fellows Elections'. *Econometrica* 71: 399–407.

Harrison, Glenn W. and List, John A. 2004. 'Field Experiments'. *Journal of Economic Literature* 42: 1009–55.

Hensher David A. and Johnson, Lester W. 1981. *Applied Discrete Choice Modelling*. London: Croom Helm.

Hirsch, Fred. 1976. *The Social Limits of Growth*. Cambridge, MA: Harvard University Press.

Holden, Anthony. 1994. *Behind the Oscar: The Secret History of the Academy Awards*. New York: Plume.

Holmström, Bengt and Milgrom, Paul. 1991. 'Multitask Principal–Agent Analyses: Incentive Contracts, Asset Ownership, and Job Design'. *Journal of Law, Economics, and Organisation* 7: 24–52.

House of Commons. 2004. *A Matter of Honour: Reforming the Honours System. Fifth Report of Session 2003–04. Volume I*. London: Stationery Office.

Huberman, Bernardo A., Loch, Christoph H., and Önçüler, Ayse. 2004. 'Status as a Valued Resource'. *Social Psychology Quarterly* 67: 103–14.

Huffman, David and Bognanno, Michael. 2015. 'Performance Pay and Workers' Non-Monetary Motivations: Evidence from a Natural Experiment'. Unpublished paper, University of Oxford and IZA.

Hustinx, Lesley, Cnaan, Ram A., and Handy, Femida. 2010. 'Navigating Theories of Volunteering: A Hybrid Map for a Complex Phenomenon'. *Journal for the Theory of Social Behaviour* 40: 410–34.

Jeffrey, Scott. 2004. 'The Benefits of Tangible Non-Monetary Incentives'. Working Paper, University of Chicago.

Jeffrey, Scott A. and Shaffer, Victoria. 2007. 'The Motivational Properties of Tangible Incentives'. *Compensation Benefits Review* 39: 44–50.

Jeppesen, Lars Bo and Lakhani, Karim R. 2010. 'Marginality and Problem-Solving Effectiveness in Broadcast Search'. *Organisation Science* 21: 1016–33.

Kay, Sir John. 2010. *Obliquity: How Our Goals are Best Pursued Indirectly.* London: Profile Books.

Kohn, Alfie. 1999. *Punished By Rewards: The Trouble with Gold Stars, Incentive Plans, A's, Praise, and other Bribes.* Boston, MA: Houghton Mifflin.

Koutsobinas, Theodore. 2014. *The Political Economy of Status. Superstars, Markets and Culture Change.* Cheltenham, UK; Northampton, MA: Edward Elgar Publishing.

Kosfeld, Michael and Neckermann, Susanne. 2011. 'Getting More Work for Nothing? Symbolic Awards and Worker Performance'. *American Economic Journal: Microeconomics* 3: 86–99.

Kovács, Balázs and Sharkey, Amanda. 2014. 'The Paradox of Publicity: How Awards can Negatively Affect the Evaluation of Quality'. *Administrative Science Quarterly* 59: 1–33.

Kube, Sebastian, Maréchal, André Michel, and Puppe, Clemens. 2012. 'The Currency of Reciprocity: Gift Exchange in the Workplace'. *American Economic Review* 102: 1644–62.

Lacetera, Nicola. 2016. 'Incentives for Prosocial Activities'. IZA World of Labor 238. doi:10.15185/izawol.238 (accessed 27 February 2017).

Lacetera, Nicola and Macis, Mario, 2010. 'Do All Material Incentives for Pro-Social Activities Backfire? The Response to Cash and Non-Cash Incentives for Blood Donations'. *Journal of Economic Psychology* 31: 738–48.

Lange, Donald, Lee, Peggy M., and Dai, Ye. 2011. 'Organisational Reputation: A Review'. *Journal of Management* 37: 153–84.

Larkin, Ian. 2011. 'Paying $30,000 for a Gold Star: An Empirical Investigation into the Value of Peer Recognition to Software Salespeople'. Unpublished working paper.

Larkin, Ian, Pierce, Lamar, and Gino, Francesca. 2012. 'The Psychological Costs of Pay-for-Performance: Implications for the Strategic Compensation of Employees'. *Strategic Management Journal* 33: 1194–214.

Layard, Richard. 2011. *Happiness: Lessons from a New Science* (2nd edn). New York: Penguin.

Lazear, Edward P. and Rosen, Sherwin. 1981. 'Rank-Order Tournaments as Optimum Labor Contracts'. *Journal of Political Economy* 89: 841–64.

References

Lepper, Mark R., Greene, David, and Nisbett, Richard E. 1973. 'Undermining Children's Intrinsic Interest with Extrinsic Reward: A Test of the "Overjustification" Hypothesis'. *Journal of Personality and Social Psychology* 28: 129–37.

Levine, David K. 1998. 'Modeling Altruism and Spitefulness in Experiments'. *Review of Economic Dynamics* 1: 593–622.

Levitt, Steven D. and List, John A. 2009. 'Field Experiments in Economics: The Past, the Present, and the Future'. *European Economic Review* 53: 1–18.

Levy, Emanuel. 1987. *And the Winner is . . . The History and Politics of the Oscar Awards*. New York: Ungar.

Lindenberg, Siegwart. 1996. 'Continuities in the Theory of Social Production Functions'. In *Verklarende Sociologie: Opstellen Voor Reinhard Wippler*, Ganzeboom, Harry B. and Lindenberg, Siegwart (eds). Amsterdam: Thela Thesis, 169–84.

Lindenberg, Siegwart. 2013. 'Social Rationality, Self-Regulation, and Well-Being: The Regulatory Significance of Needs, Goals, and the Self'. In *Handbook of Rational Choice Social Research*, Wittek, Rafael, Snijders, Tom A. B., and Nee, Victor (eds). Stanford, CA: Stanford University Press, 72–112.

List, John A. 2007. 'On the Interpretation of Giving in Dictator Games'. *Journal of Political Economy* 115: 482–93.

List, John A. 2011. 'The Market for Charitable Giving'. *Journal of Economic Perspectives* 25: 157–80.

List, John A., Shaikh, Azeem M., and Xu, Yang. 2016. 'Multiple Hypothesis Testing in Experimental Economics'. NBER Working Paper No. 21875.

Macduff, Nancy. 2005. 'Societal Changes and the Rise of the Episodic Volunteer'. ARNOVA Occasional Paper Series, *Emerging Areas of Volunteering*, 1: 51–64.

McFadden, Daniel. 2001. 'Economic Choices?' *American Economic Review* 91(3): 351–78.

Magnus, Margaret. 1981. 'Employee Recognition: A Key to Motivation'. *Personnel Journal* 60: 103–7.

Malcomson, James M. 2012. 'Relational Incentive Contracts'. In *Handbook of Organisational Economics*, Gibbons, Robert and Roberts, John (eds). Princeton, NJ: Princeton University Press, 1014–65.

Malmendier, Ulrike and Tate, Geoffrey. 2009. 'Superstar Ceos'. *Quarterly Journal of Economics* 124: 1593–638.

Markham, Steven E., Scott, K. Dow, and McKee, Gail H. 2002. 'Recognizing Good Attendance: A Longitudinal Quasi-Experimental Field Study'. *Personnel Psychology* 55: 639–60.

Medvec, Victoria Husted, Madey, Scott F., and Gilovich, Thomas. 1995. 'When Less is More: Counterfactual Thinking and Satisfaction Among Olympic Medalists'. *Journal of Personality and Social Psychology* 69: 603–10.

Merton, Robert K. 1968. 'The Matthew Effect in Science'. *Science* 159: 56–63.

Mishel, Lawrence and Davis, Alyssa. 2014. 'CEO Pay Continues to Rise as Typical Workers are Paid Less'. Economic Policy Institute, Issue Brief 380. http://www.epi.org/files/2014/ceo-pay-continues-to-rise.pdf (accessed 27 February 2017).

Moser, Petra and Nicholas, Tom. 2013. 'Prizes, Publicity and Patents: Non-Monetary Awards as a Mechanism to Encourage Innovation'. *Journal of Industrial Economics* 61: 763–88.

Mueller, Dennis C. 1997. *Perspectives on Public Choice: A Handbook*. New York: Cambridge University Press.

Mueller, Dennis C. 2003. *Public Choice III*. Cambridge: Cambridge University Press.

Murray, Fiona, Stern, Scott, Campbell, Georgina, and Maccormack, Alan. 2012. 'Grand Innovation Prizes: A Theoretical, Normative, and Empirical Evaluation'. *Research Policy* 41: 1779–92.

Neckermann, Susanne. 2009. 'Of Awards in Companies: An Econometric Assessment of Honor and Recognition as Incentives'. Dissertation, University of Zurich.

Neckermann, Susanne and Frey, Bruno S. 2013. 'And the Winner is...? The Motivating Power of Employee Awards'. *Journal of Socio-Economics* 46: 66–77.

Neckermann, Susanne, Cueni, Reto, and Frey, Bruno S. 2014. 'Awards at Work'. *Labour Economics* 31: 205–17.

Nelson, Bob. 2012. *1001 Ways to Reward Your Employees*. New York: Workman Publishing.

Nelson, Randy A., Donihue, Michael R., Waldman, Donald M., and Wheaton, Calbraith. 2001. 'What's an Oscar Worth?' *Economic Inquiry* 39: 1–6.

Nickerson, Jack A. and Zenger, Todd R. 2008. 'Envy, Comparison Costs, and the Economic Theory of the Firm'. *Strategic Management Journal* 29: 1429–49.

Non, Arjan. 2012. 'Gift-Exchange, Incentives, and Heterogeneous Workers'. *Games and Economic Behaviour* 75: 319–36.

Osterloh, Margit and Frey, Bruno S. 2000. 'Motivation, Knowledge Transfer, and Organisational Forms'. *Organisation Science* 11: 538–50.

Piketty, Thomas. 2014. *Capital in the Twenty-First Century*. Cambridge, MA: Harvard University Press.

Piketty, Thomas and Saez, Emmanuel. 2003. 'Income Inequality in the United States, 1913–1998'. *Quarterly Journal of Economics* 118: 1–39.

Piketty, Thomas and Saez, Emmanuel. 2013. 'Top Incomes and the Great Recession: Recent Evolutions and Policy Implications'. *IMF Economic Review* 61: 456–78.

Pink, Daniel H. 2011. *Drive: The Surprising Truth About What Motivates Us*. New York: Penguin.

Ponzo, Michela and Scoppa, Vincenzo. 2015. 'Experts' Awards and Economic Success: Evidence from an Italian Literary Prize'. *Journal of Cultural Economics* 39: 1–27.

Rablen, Matthew D. and Oswald, Andrew J. 2008. 'Mortality and Immortality: The Nobel Prize as an Experiment into the Effect of Status upon Longevity'. *Journal of Health Economics* 27: 1462–71.

Redelmeier, Donald A. and Singh, Sheldon M. 2001a. 'Survival in Academy Award-Winning Actors and Actresses'. *Annals of Internal Medicine* 134: 955–62.

Redelmeier, Donald A. and Singh, Sheldon M. 2001b. 'Longevity of Screenwriters Who Win an Academy Award: Longitudinal Study'. *British Medical Journal* 323: 1491–6.

Resnick, Paul, Kuwabara, Ko, Zeckhauser, Richard, and Friedman, Eric. 2000. 'Reputation Systems'. *Communications of the ACM* 43: 45–8.

Restivo, Michael and van de Rijt, Arnout. 2012. 'Experimental Study of Informal Rewards in Peer Production'. *PLoS ONE* 7: e34358.

Restivo, Michael and van de Rijt, Arnout. 2014. 'No Praise without Effort: Experimental Evidence on How Rewards Affect Wikipedia's Contributor Community'. *Information, Communication & Society* 17: 451–62.

Riley, John G. 2001. 'Silver Signals: Twenty-Five Years of Screening and Signaling'. *Journal of Economic Literature* 39: 432–78.

Risk, James C. 1972. *The History of the Order of the Bath and its Insignia*. London: Spink & Son.

Robertson, Megan C. 2010. 'Medals of the World'. http://www.medals.org.uk/ (accessed June 2014).

Rosen, Sherwin. 1981. 'The Economics of Superstars'. *American Economic Review* 71: 845–58.

Rossi, Peter H. and Anderson Andy B. 1982. 'The Factorial Survey Approach: An Introduction'. In *Measuring Social Judgments: The Factorial Survey Approach*, Rossi Peter H. and Nock Steven L. (eds). Beverly Hills: Sage, 15–67.

Rothschild, Michael and Stiglitz, Joseph. 1976. 'Equilibrium in Competitive Insurance Markets: An Essay on the Economics of Imperfect Information'. *Quarterly Journal of Economics* 90: 629–49.

Rousseau, Denise M. 1989. 'Psychological and Implied Contracts in Organisations'. *Employee Responsibilities and Rights Journal* 2: 121–39.

Scitovsky, Tibor. 1976. *The Joyless Economy: An Inquiry into Human Satisfaction and Consumer Dissatisfaction*. New York: Oxford University Press.

Siming, Linus. 2016. 'Orders of Merit and CEO Compensation: Evidence from a Natural Experiment'. *Corporate Governance* 24: 64–78.

Singer-Vine, Jeremy. 2011. 'Decorated Officer: An Interactive Guide to all the Stars, Medals, and Ribbons on the Uniform of Gen. David Petraeus'. *Slate*, 18 May.

Snyder, Mark and Omoto, Allen M. 2008. 'Volunteerism: Social Issues Perspectives and Social Policy Implications'. *Social Issues and Policy Review* 2: 1–36.

Sobel, Dava. 1995. *Longitude: The True Story of a Lone Genius Who Solved the Greatest Scientific Problem of His Time*. New York: Walker & Company.

Stiglitz, Joseph E. 2000. 'The Contributions of the Economics of Information to Twentieth-Century Economics'. *Quarterly Journal of Economics* 115: 1441–78.

Stiglitz, Joseph E. 2001. 'Prize Lecture: Information and the Change in the Paradigm in Economics'. In *Les Prix Nobel. The Nobel Prizes 2001*, Frängsmyr, Tore (ed.). Stockholm: The Nobel Foundation, 472–540.

Stocqueler, Joachim Hayward. 1853. *The Titles, Honours, and Descent of the Duke*. London: Ingram, Cooke, and Co.

Stutzer, Alois. 2004. 'The Role of Income Aspirations in Individual Happiness'. *Journal of Economic Behaviour and Organisation* 54: 89–109.

Suazo, Mark M., Martínez, Patricia G., and Sandoval, Rudy. 2009. 'Creating Psychological and Legal Contracts through Human Resource Practices: A Signaling Theory Perspective'. *Human Resource Management Review* 19: 154–66.

Suh, Bongwon, Convertino, Gregorio, Chi, Ed H., and Pirolli, Peter. 2009. 'The Singularity is Not Near: Slowing Growth of Wikipedia'. P. 5th International Symposium on Wikis and Open Collaboration: 8.

Telegraph, The. 2010. 'Gen. David Petraeus and His Medals'. 9 June.

Tise, Larry E. 2014. *Mega Awards, Challenge Prizes, and Calculating the Prestige of the World's Greatest Awards—the Stakes are Getting Higher.* Philadelphia: International Congress of Distinguished Awards.

Tran, Anh and Zeckhauser, Richard. 2012. 'Rank as an Inherent Incentive: Evidence from a Field Experiment'. *Journal of Public Economics* 96: 645–50.

Tripnaux, Eric. 2008. *L'origine de l'ordre de Léopold.* Brussels: Société de l'Ordre de Léopold.

Wade, James B., Porac, Joseph F., Pollock, Timothy G., and Graffin, Scott D. 2006. 'The Burden of Celebrity: The Impact of CEO Certification Contests on CEO Pay and Performance'. *Academy of Management Journal* 49: 643–60.

Weibel, Antoinette, Rost, Katja, and Osterloh, Margit. 2010. 'Pay for Performance in the Public Sector – Benefits and (Hidden) Costs'. *Journal of Public Administration Research and Theory* 20: 387–412.

Weigelt, Keith and Camerer, Colin. 1988. 'Reputation and Corporate Strategy: A Review of Recent Theory and Applications'. *Strategic Management Journal* 9: 443–54.

Weisbrod, Burton A. and Hansen, W. Lee. 1972. 'Toward a General Theory of Awards, or, Do Economists Need a Hall of Fame?' *Journal of Political Economy* 80: 422–31.

Wikipedia. 'Declining British Honours' https://en.wikipedia.org/wiki/List_of_people_who_have_declined_a_British_honour (accessed 27 February 2017).

Wikipedia. 'List of Prizes, Medals, and Awards' https://en.wikipedia.org/wiki/List_of_prizes,_medals_and_awards (accessed 27 February 2017).

Women and Wikimedia Survey. 2011. Wikimedia, Meta-Wiki. https://meta.wikimedia.org/wiki/Women_and_Wikimedia_Survey 2011 (accessed 27 February 2017).

Zahavi, Amotz. 1975. 'Mate Selection: A Selection for a Handicap'. *Journal of Theoretical Biology* 53: 205–14.

Zuckerman, Harriet. 1992. 'The Proliferation of Prizes: Nobel Complements and Nobel Surrogates in the Reward System of Science'. *Theoretical Medicine* 13: 217–31.

Zuckerman, Harriet. 1996. *Scientific Elite: Nobel Laureates in the United States.* Brunswick, NJ: Transaction Publishers.

Author Index

Subject Index